JUNIOR ILLUSTRATED ENCYCLOPEDIA
NATURE

JUNIOR ILLUSTRATED ENCYCLOPEDIA

NATURE

MARTYN BRAMWELL

Kingfisher Books

First published in paperback in
1991 by Kingfisher Books.
Originally published in hardback
in 1988 by
Grisewood & Dempsey Ltd,
Elsley House,
24–30 Great Titchfield Street,
London W1P 7AD.

**British Library Cataloguing in
Publication Data**
Bramwell, Martyn *1944–*
    Nature.
    1. Natural history
    I. Title
    508

    ISBN 0-86272-763-4

Editor
Ann Kay
Design
Ben White
Illustrations
Jeane Colville
Jeremy Gower
Ian Jackson
Andrew Macdonald
Kevin Maddison
Janos Marffy/
Thorogood Burgess Agency
Alan Male/
Linden Artists' Agency
David Wright/
Thorogood Burgess Agency

Printed and bound in Spain
by Graficas Reunidas

Contents

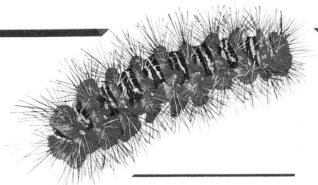

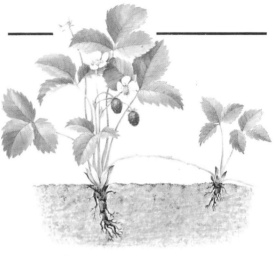

Introduction

Understanding the world of nature

One way or another, we have been studying biology for several million years. Long before they could speak, let alone write, primitive people were studying plants and animals, learning which nuts and berries and roots were good to eat and discovering which kinds of animals could be caught and eaten and which were to be avoided. At this stage it was hardly a science, but we were already classifying living things into groups, and studying their behaviour.

Below: *Earth has more than a million different animal species – and over 700,000 of them are insects. They come in every imaginable size and shape and colour, and are found in almost every habitat on Earth.*

Serious study of the living world goes back to the great civilizations of China and the Mediterranean lands. More than 2300 years ago, the Greek philosopher Aristotle wrote a famous encyclopedia of nature which included many descriptions of animal and bird migration and his ideas about what caused them.

Much later, in 1753, the great Swedish botanist Carl von Linnaeus gave the world the first scientific method for naming animals and plants. He gave each one a pair of names that would belong to that animal or plant and to no other. So, the scientific name of the lion is *Panthera leo*; that of the other great cat, the tiger, is *Panthera tigris*. The same system works for plants. The beautiful American sugar maple is called *Acer saccharum*, while its European cousin the sycamore is *Acer pseudoplatanus*.

There are two other great milestones along the road of learning. In 1859 Charles Darwin published his theory of evolution. It caused the most enormous arguments at the time, but in many ways it was the start of truly scientific modern biology. And then as recently as 1953, James Watson and Francis Crick discovered the chemical code that makes evolution and everything else possible. That code was the spiral chemical called DNA. It is a living blue-print – a master-plan that is different for each animal or plant. It is the DNA blueprint that makes an elephant different from a mouse. It is the DNA blueprint that can produce a million identical buttercups in a field. And it is DNA that makes us all so similar – yet at the same time all so different in countless tiny details.

Below: *By producing seeds, and many different ways of scattering them over the land, plants were able to spread outwards from the primitive swamps and river banks and cover almost the entire Earth.*

Below: *The dormouse is one of Europe's smallest animals. It lives in the tangled undergrowth beneath hedges and in thickets, and is active mainly at night.*

1. The Living Earth

The story of the Earth begins more than 4600 million years ago in a huge cloud of dust and gas spinning slowly through space. Gradually, this dust and gas became concentrated at the centre of the cloud, and as more particles were pulled in by a force called gravity, the pressure and temperature rose higher and higher. Finally the heat and pressure reached the point at which chemical reactions gave birth to a new star – the Sun.

At the same time, parts of the original cloud farther out from the centre began to form smaller concentrations. These would later become the nine planets of the Sun's family – the solar system. Just how the different planets formed depended on how close they were to the fierce heat of the Sun. The inner planets – Mercury, Venus, Earth and Mars – eventually became rock. Most of their gases were driven off by the Sun's heat. The outer planets – Jupiter, Saturn, Uranus and Neptune – remained cold. Now they are gigantic freezing worlds of dense gas, while tiny Pluto probably consists mainly of ice.

As the Earth began to form, its collapsing mass of dust particles melted, and the planet became a glowing ball of molten rock, wrapped in a poisonous 'atmosphere' – a mixture of the gases hydrogen, carbon dioxide, methane and ammonia. Slowly it cooled, and a thin 'crust' of solid rock developed – torn by earthquakes and volcanoes. The constant eruptions added more and more steamy water vapour to the atmosphere until, about 4000 million years ago, enough water had collected for clouds to form and rain to fall. Violent storms lashed the primitive landscape and swollen rivers started to fill the first great lakes and seas. There was still no sign of life – but the stage was set.

Right: *The story of the Earth begins thousands of millions of years ago in a dense cloud of dust and gas spinning through the blackness of space.*
Below: *Earth is near the middle of the* **ecosphere** – *the zone around the Sun in which it is neither too hot nor too cold for life.*
Words in **bold** *refer to glossary entries.*

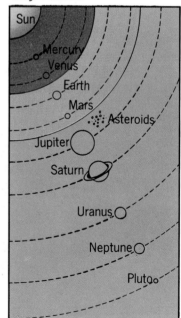

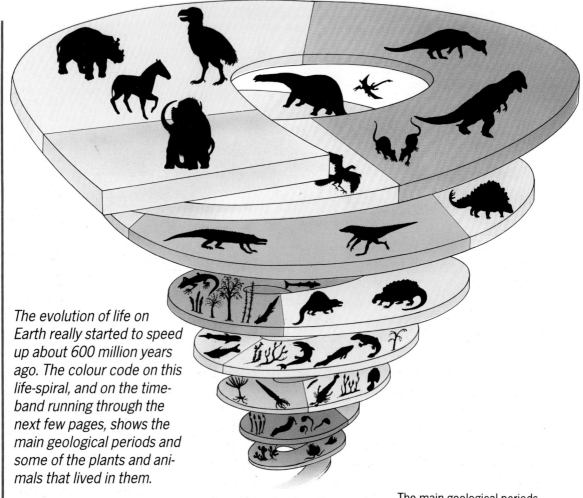

The evolution of life on Earth really started to speed up about 600 million years ago. The colour code on this life-spiral, and on the time-band running through the next few pages, shows the main geological periods and some of the plants and animals that lived in them.

The story of life

For the first thousand million years or so there was no life at all on Earth. There was no oxygen, and the first **cell** had not yet appeared. But the seas were rich in dissolved minerals. Some came straight from volcanoes on the sea-bed while others were washed out of rocks on land and carried into the seas by rivers. Over millions of years these minerals joined together in countless new and different combinations.

Eventually a rather unusual kind of chemical group, or **molecule**, appeared on the scene. It was unusual because as well as obtaining energy from the chemicals in the water around it, it could also use those chemicals to make exact copies of itself. In other words, it could reproduce. These were the first living cells, and they probably appeared about 3000 million years ago.

Evolution is a slow process, and hundreds of millions of years passed before the next big breakthrough. Then, some of the more complicated cells in the ancient seas started to make a green chemical called **chlorophyll**. The

The main geological periods and when they started (dates in millions of years ago).

1. Quaternary 2 mya
2. Tertiary 65 mya
3. Cretaceous 140 mya
4. Jurassic 195 mya
5. Triassic 230 mya
6. Permian 280 mya
7. Carboniferous 345 mya
8. Devonian 395 mya
9. Silurian 435 mya
10. Ordovician 500 mya
11. Cambrian 570 mya

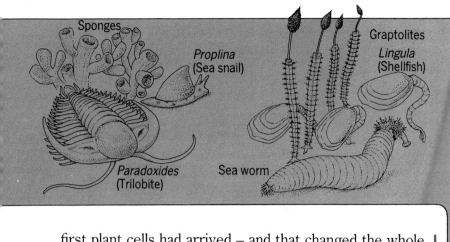

Sponges
Proplina
(Sea snail)
Graptolites
Lingula
(Shellfish)
Paradoxides
(Trilobite)
Sea worm

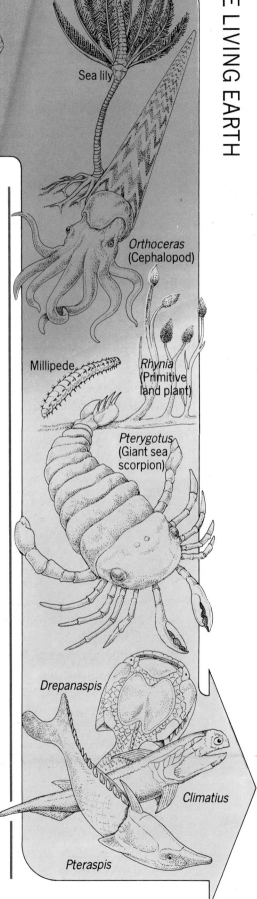

Sea lily
Orthoceras
(Cephalopod)
Millipede
Rhynia
(Primitive
land plant)
Pterygotus
(Giant sea
scorpion)
Drepanaspis
Climatius
Pteraspis

first plant cells had arrived – and that changed the whole world. The chlorophyll enabled these cells to capture the energy in the Sun's rays, and using that energy they were able to make their own food supplies from the water and carbon dioxide around them. During this process, the plants gave off oxygen. At first, all the oxygen produced by these simple, single-celled plants was soaked up by the rocks of the Earth's crust, but soon it began to accumulate in the atmosphere, slowly turning that poisonous mixture of gases into life-giving air.

By about 1000 million years ago, the simple plant life of the oceans had paved the way for animal life to appear. Once again it was a slow process. The first animals were tiny single-celled creatures, probably very like some of those we find in sea and pond water today. We know very little about them, or about many of those that came later, because they had no hard parts – no skeletons or shells – and so they were not preserved in the Earth's rocks as **fossils**. But by about 600 million years ago many new kinds of animal were appearing. They spread and multiplied at a staggering rate.

Life in the ancient seas

Faint fossils of very simple plants and primitive worm-like animals have been found in rocks up to 3000 million years old, but the main fossil story starts about 600 million years ago at the dawn of the Cambrian period. At this time the land was still completely bare, without a sign of life, but the seas were already teeming with life. As well as a host of different seaweeds there were sponges and jellyfish, sea urchins and shellfish of all kinds. More than 1500 different animal **species** have been found in rocks of this age, and all are invertebrates – that is, animals with no backbone. One of the most interesting animals of this time was the trilobite – shown at the top of this page. It was a distant relative of the spiders, crabs and lobsters of today.

In the Ordovician period (500–435 million years ago) many more swimming animals appeared, including a group called the 'cephalopods'. These ancient relatives of the

When a bony or shelled animal dies in a lake or sea, its soft fleshy parts rot away or are eaten by other animals. But if the skeleton or shell is buried fairly quickly under mud or sand there is a good chance that it will be preserved as a fossil.

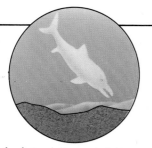

1. Animal dies and sinks to the sea- or lake-bed

2. Hard parts become buried under sand, silt or mud

3. Bones are slowly replaced by hard mineral crystals

octopus and squid lived in shells – some tightly coiled, others long and straight. There were also many new kinds of coral, starfish, sea lily and other creatures.

The first animals with backbones also appeared at this time. They were primitive fishes. The earliest ones had no jaws. Instead, their mouths were specialized for scraping and sucking, rather like a modern lamprey. But many of the fishes that came later, in the Silurian period (435–395 million years ago) and the Devonian (395–345 m.y. ago) were massive creatures. Some were up to nine metres long, with armoured bodies and powerful jaws. With these monsters, and giant sea scorpions up to two metres long, the ancient seas must have been full of danger for the smaller animals.

Moving on to the land

During the final part of the Silurian period several important things happened. Firstly, plants moved out on to dry land. The first ones were simply modified seaweeds, but specialized land plants with strong upright stems soon developed. Animals, too, finally left the safety of the seas. The first to take to dry land were probably some of the smaller scorpions and millipedes.

The short Devonian period is often called the 'Age of the Fishes' and it is true that at this time there was a huge increase in the number and variety of fish. But it was also the time when primitive trees began to clothe the land in forests of ferns and **conifers**. Spiders and insects made their appearance, and along the shores the first **amphibians** evolved. These were the first four-legged land animals – the vital link between the fishes and the true land animals that were soon to follow.

The age of the great coal forests

In the Carboniferous period (345–280 million years ago) huge forests covered large parts of the Earth. Many new

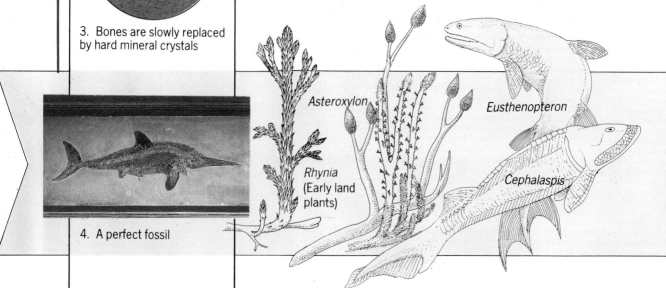

4. A perfect fossil

Asteroxylon

Rhynia (Early land plants)

Eusthenopteron

Cephalaspis

plants evolved, including palm-like cycads and strange clubmosses, and the trees and undergrowth sheltered spiders, millipedes and giant dragonflies with wings spanning 70 centimetres. In the wet swamp-forests, dead trees and piles of rotting vegetation built up year after year and were later buried under thick layers of sand and mud. Now, after millions of years of crushing and squeezing, the remains of these ancient swamps are thick seams of coal, mined to fuel our power stations and factories.

During this period the climate in many parts of the world became drier, and many more new species appeared, including the very first **reptiles**. This remarkable group of animals evolved from the amphibians, but they were much better equipped for success. They laid much tougher eggs than the amphibians, and because they could lay their eggs on dry land instead of having to lay them in, or at least close to, water, they could spread out over much greater areas. The arrival of the reptiles set the scene for animals to complete their take-over of the land.

The age of the reptiles

Some reptiles, such as the fin-backed lizards of the Permian period (280–230 million years ago) were specially adapted for life in desert regions. Others were designed for life in swamp forests or open grasslands, woodlands or rivers and lakes. The reptiles ruled the Earth for a total of 140 million years – through the Triassic (230–195), Jurassic (195–140) and Cretaceous (140–65 million years

The time-band shown here covers the period roughly from 400 to 250 million years ago. It was a time of great change. Primitive forests covered huge areas of land, and the first true land animals appeared.

Dimetrodon
(Flesh-eater)

(Fin-backed reptiles)

Edaphosaurus
(Plant-eater)

Hylonomus
(One of the first reptiles)

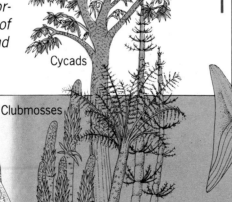

Cycads

Clubmosses

Horsetails

Cladoselache

Ichthyostega
(An early amphibian)

Pleuracanthus
(Primitive sharks)

13

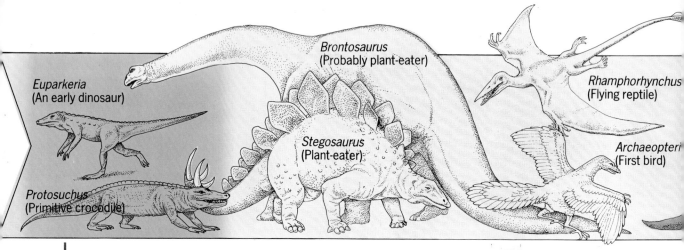

Euparkeria
(An early dinosaur)

Brontosaurus
(Probably plant-eater)

Rhamphorhynchus
(Flying reptile)

Stegosaurus
(Plant-eater)

Archaeopteri
(First bird)

Protosuchus
(Primitive crocodile)

CHARLES DARWIN (1809–1882)

As a young man, Charles Darwin spent five years at sea as naturalist on board *HMS Beagle*. The ship's voyage of scientific discovery took it right around the world, and Darwin was fascinated by the enormous number and variety of animals and plants he saw, and by the fossils he discovered. He came to the conclusion that animals and plants change gradually over long periods of time and that modern species are descended from the animals and plants of long ago.

Darwin spent the rest of his life working on his theories of how one kind of animal could develop from another. His main theory was called **natural selection**. Darwin realized that the young animals in each generation were very similar but that they did have slight variations – for example, in size or colour. He also knew that these characteristics came from the parents and could be passed on to the next generation. His idea was that in each generation the individuals that were best equipped for their environment would be the ones who would survive, breed successfully, and so pass on their useful characteristics to the next generation. Over millions of years this slow process of change could produce animals very different indeed from their far distant ancestors.

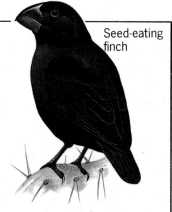

Seed-eating finch

Above: *Each of the 13 species of finch on the Galapagos Islands has a different bill shape – specially suited to a particular kind of food. Seed-eaters have big powerful bills. Insect-eaters have slender pointed bills. One species (see p.16) has even learned to use a tool.*

The animals on the left show three different aspects of natural selection. Twig-like colour and shape improve the stick insect's chance of survival. The bat succeeds because it is highly specialized in many ways. The bird of paradise will succeed in finding a mate because when he displays his feathers fully he looks much more impressive than his rivals.

Stick insect

Bird of Paradise

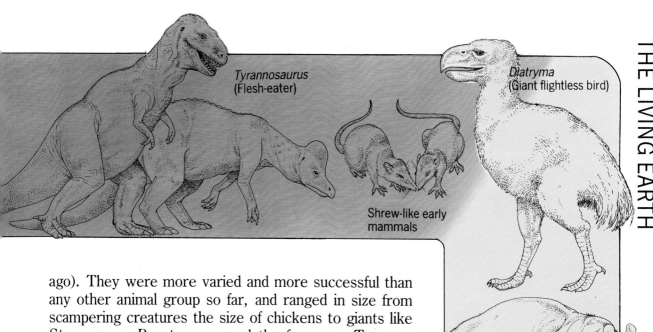

Tyrannosaurus
(Flesh-eater)

Shrew-like early
mammals

Diatryma
(Giant flightless bird)

Uintatherium

Mesohippus
(Early form of horse)

Woolly Mammoth

ago). They were more varied and more successful than any other animal group so far, and ranged in size from scampering creatures the size of chickens to giants like *Stegosaurus*, *Brontosaurus* and the fearsome *Tyrannosaurus*. There were all kinds of plant-eaters and flesh-eaters, fliers, runners and swimmers, and during their long reign they produced the ancestors of two of the most advanced animal groups of the modern world – the mammals and the birds.

Some time during the Jurassic period, small shrew-like insect-eating animals appeared. They were the first primitive **mammals**. And towards the end of this period a rather strange 'flying reptile' appeared in the marshy forests. In many ways it was still a reptile, but it had a remarkable new feature – feathers. It probably could not fly very well, but this crow-sized creature, *Archaeopteryx*, was the ancestor of all our modern birds – from robins and toucans to eagles and ostriches.

The mammals take over
About 65 million years ago, the age of the reptiles came to an end. Most scientists believe that they died out because of sudden changes in the climate. Whatever the real cause, the great beasts disappeared forever and their place was taken by the mammals. These were warm-blooded animals. Most gave birth to live young instead of laying eggs, and above all they were very adaptable. They specialized in every imaginable **habitat** and life-style, and very quickly became the ruling animal group.

Many of the early mammals were very different from those we know today. There were giant long-haired ground sloths up to six metres long, and long-legged camel-like animals with short elephant-like trunks. Many of these species did not last long. Soon, more familiar shapes began to appear, and before long the forests and grasslands were taken over by horses and antelopes, mice and squirrels, elephants, monkeys – and the ancestors of modern man.

A world of specialists

The process of natural selection 'tailors' each animal or plant to a particular position, or 'niche' in the natural world. Each niche is rather like a job description. Imagine, for example, an advertisement for a small burrowing insect-eater. The mole would probably fill that vacancy. Every habitat is made up of dozens of these niches. Even a small city garden provides a wide range of niches – from animals that help to make use of dead leaves (earth-worms and woodlice) to hunters like owls and cats.

Usually a niche is filled by exactly the kind of animal you would expect. But not always. Madagascar, for example, has no native woodpeckers, but the 'woodpecker' way of life is filled by a curious little animal called an aye-aye. Just like a woodpecker, this animal has special adaptations that enable it to feed on the grubs and larvae (plural of **larva**) that infest dead and decaying wood. In the same way, Australia has lots of **marsupials** (pouched mammals) and rather fewer ordinary mammals (**placentals**) and so the marsupials have taken over many of the niches normally filled by placentals. The job of anteater, for example, is filled by the numbat, a marsupial, while the job of grassland grazer is filled by kangaroos. Zebras and antelopes fill this particular niche in Africa while the llamas do the same job in the highland grasslands of South America.

Successes and failures

Over millions of years of evolution, some animal designs have been more successful than others. Many animals and plants have become extinct. The mighty *Tyrannosaurus* and the fast-swimming, ocean-going *Elasmosaurus* both died out. So did the giant ground sloth and, more recently, the woolly mammoth. But other designs worked so well that they lasted for many millions of years. The tuatara of

Below: *The familiar wood-peckers of Europe and America have sharp power-ful bills for breaking up de-caying wood, and long sticky tongues for pulling out the grubs on which they feed. In Hawaii the same niche is filled by the sharp-billed akiapolaau. On the Galapagos Islands the woodpecker finch uses a cactus spine to poke out grubs, while in Madagascar the aye-aye, and in Australia the striped possum, both use long, thin sharp-clawed fingers for the same task.*

Striped possum

European woodpecker

Akiapolaau

Woodpecker finch

Aye-aye

New Zealand is an unusual modern lizard that seems to have hardly changed at all in the last 200 million years. The coelacanth, too, was thought to have been extinct for 70 million years – until a living specimen was pulled up in a fisherman's net in the Indian Ocean in 1938.

Winning designs

Each particular animal design is nature's answer to a design problem, and one of the curious things about evolution is that the same design often crops up at opposite ends of the world – even in unrelated animals. The kit fox of North America and the fennec fox of North Africa are almost identical. So are the gerbil of Africa, the kangaroo rat of North America and the jerboa of Asia. All have special adaptations for life in desert regions.

Even more dramatic are the cases of quite unrelated animals being 'designed' to fill the same niches – like some of the South American hummingbirds and giant moths. These very different creatures are roughly the same size, and both feed by hovering and sipping nectar from the deep trumpet-shaped flowers of certain forest trees.

Tuatara

Coelacanth

Left: The tuatara of New Zealand, the coelacanth of the Indian Ocean and the king crab of North America have remained almost unchanged for many millions of years.

Horseshoe (King) crab

Elasmosaurus

Right: The great sea reptiles of the Triassic period (such as Elasmosaurus)*, and many of the early mammals (for example* Megatherium)*, failed to adapt to a constantly changing world.*

Megatherium

The desert foxes are quick and agile lightweights with large ears to help them get rid of body heat. The desert rodents have long, kangaroo-like legs to keep them high off the hot sand, and long tails that help them balance when hopping. Both foxes and rodents shelter in burrows by day and feed mainly in the cool evening and early morning.

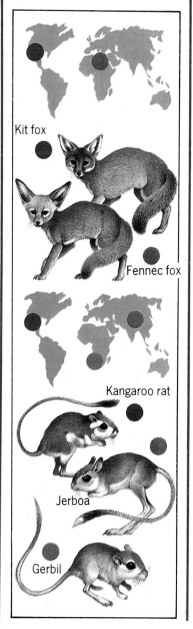

Kit fox

Fennec fox

Kangaroo rat

Jerboa

Gerbil

17

Below: *Selection in action – peppered moths can be silver-grey or very dark in colour. Originally the pale kind was most common because it was well camouflaged when at rest on trees covered in silvery lichen. The darker moths showed up and so were easy prey for birds. But earlier this century, the dark variety became common in industrial areas because it was less easily seen on trees that had lost their lichen due to air pollution.*

Now, with cleaner air, the lichen is returning and the pale moths are once again becoming quite common.

Living partnerships

In the natural world there are many specialized partnerships in which two animals, or two plants, or a plant and an animal live together. In some cases the partners cannot live separately: they are completely dependent on each other. In other cases the arrangement is a bit more casual. It is useful – but not essential.

Most people are familiar with the grey, green and orange lichens that grow on stonework and on tree bark. But the lichen is not just one plant. It is a combination of an alga (a simple plant of the seaweed family) and a fungus. The alga has **chlorophyll**, and so is able to use the Sun's energy to make food, while the fungus spreads its fine, root-like threads through the rock or tree bark, collecting moisture and minerals.

Many partnerships have the single purpose of making sure that flowers are 'pollinated' (see p.48–50), so that seeds can be produced to provide the next generation. Some of the best examples are found in the tropical forests, where the bills of many hummingbirds are specially shaped to fit the deep-belled flowers of their plant partners. Other plants are pollinated by flies, moths, beetles, bats or small animals. All these 'helpers' are attracted by the plant's sweet **nectar**, and all help by carrying **pollen** from one flower to another as they feed.

A more casual arrangement exists between large, cattle-like animals such as wildebeeste and a type of heron known as a cattle egret. The birds perch on the animal's back, hopping down now and then to pounce on the large

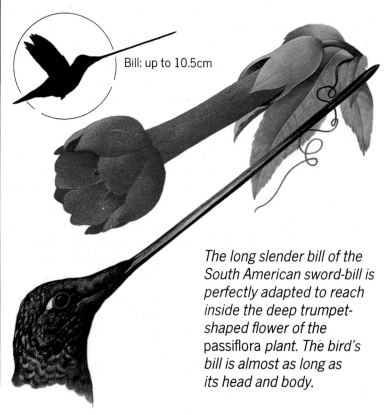

Bill: up to 10.5cm

The long slender bill of the South American sword-bill is perfectly adapted to reach inside the deep trumpet-shaped flower of the passiflora plant. The bird's bill is almost as long as its head and body.

Sifaka
(Madagascar)

The sifaka is one of many rare animals on the island of Madagascar. The kagu of New Caledonia in the Pacific Ocean has no known relatives. The kangaroo became isolated when Australia broke away from a larger land mass.

Kagu
(New Caledonia)

Kangaroo
(Australia)

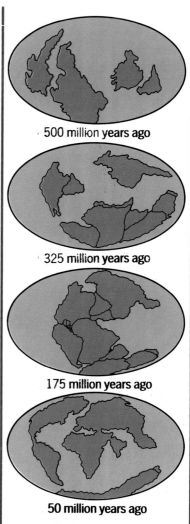

500 million **years ago**

325 million **years ago**

175 million **years ago**

50 million **years ago**

Ancient positions of the Earth's landmasses can be worked out from the shapes of the continents, and from fossils and other geological evidence. The last great break-up began about 200 million years ago – and the continents are still moving. The Atlantic Ocean, for example, is getting wider at the rate of several centimetres a year.

insects flushed from the grass by the animal's hooves. In return for this favour, the birds give a noisy warning if danger approaches.

All these arrangements benefit both partners, but there are other, less friendly, partnerships in which one partner (called a **parasite**) gets all the benefit while the other (called the **host**) gets nothing – or may even be killed. Many kinds of fungus are parasites, stealing their food from the plants they live on. Other examples are the liver flukes, worms and bacteria that live inside the bodies of larger animals, often causing sickness or even death. In the natural world every living thing must compete for survival – right down to the smallest bacteria.

Nature's castaways

We now know that the continents have not always been in their present positions. In the past they have drifted over the Earth's surface, colliding to form one huge super-continent before splitting up and drifting apart again.

Over millions of years, many animals and plants have been separated from their relatives and have continued to survive and evolve in isolation. The duck-billed platypus, for example, a primitive egg-laying mammal, was cast adrift on the huge 'raft' of Australia – and today is found nowhere else on Earth. The pouched mammals, too, survive mainly in Australia, with a few distant relatives in South America. More recently, Madagascar drifted away from Africa like a rocky Noah's ark, carrying with it the world's entire population of lemurs.

Energy, water and food

The one thing that even the simplest plant can do – but no animal can do – is to make food. That is why animal life could not evolve on Earth until after the plants had appeared. All animals eat plants, or other animals that in turn eat plants. But just what *is* plant food?

The answer to this question is hidden inside every green leaf. The leaf is the plant's food factory, and it works because of that amazing green chemical **chlorophyll**. Chlorophyll can soak up the energy in the Sun's rays and use it to power chemical processes called **photosynthesis** that turn water (from the soil) and carbon dioxide (from the air) into sugars. These sugars are the building blocks of life. They can be joined together in all sorts of

Below: *Water is always in motion over the Earth's surface. It evaporates from the surface of the sea and is picked up by warm air currents that carry it far inland. There it condenses and falls as rain and snow. Some may stay for a while in an ice-cap, glacier or lake, but sooner or later it starts its downhill journey back to the sea. This endless process is the 'water cycle'.*

Above: *All animal life depends on the food produced by green leaves, water and sunlight. The process is called 'photosynthesis' – a word meaning 'building with light'.*

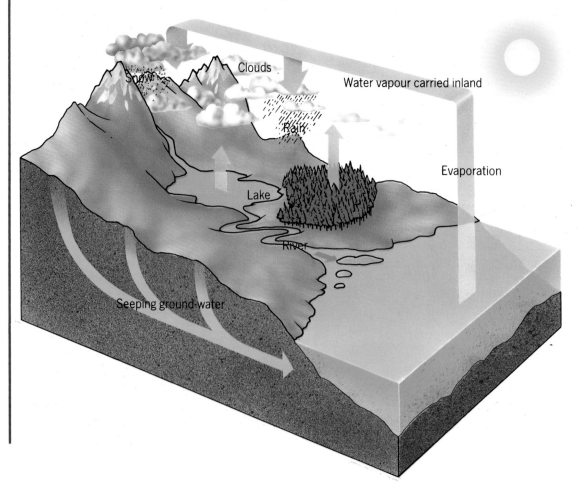

Clouds

Snow

Water vapour carried inland

Rain

Evaporation

Lake

River

Seeping ground-water

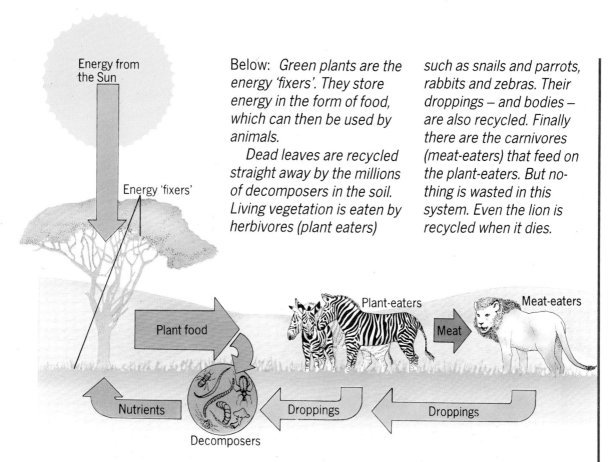

Below: *Green plants are the energy 'fixers'. They store energy in the form of food, which can then be used by animals.*

Dead leaves are recycled straight away by the millions of decomposers in the soil. Living vegetation is eaten by herbivores (plant eaters) such as snails and parrots, rabbits and zebras. Their droppings – and bodies – are also recycled. Finally there are the carnivores (meat-eaters) that feed on the plant-eaters. But nothing is wasted in this system. Even the lion is recycled when it dies.

combinations to make many different molecules. But plants and animals also need small amounts of several other chemicals in order to make petals and roots, muscles and hair, and to carry out various chemical processes. These other chemicals are called 'nutrients' and they are dissolved, in very small amounts, in the water in the soil. In places where the soil is well supplied with these essential nutrients the natural vegetation is rich, and farmland produces good crops. In places where the soil is poor, only scrub will grow, and crops are very poor.

Supplying the energy needed for plants to grow is not a problem – it pours in every day from the Sun. Nutrients, on the other hand, are an entirely different matter. The Earth already has its entire supply of carbon, oxygen, nitrogen, phosphorus, potassium, calcium and all the other minerals that are used by plants and animals. There are no new supplies, so these nutrients are used again and again and again. The process is called recycling, and it is a very efficient one.

When an animal or plant dies, its remains are slowly broken down by grubs and beetles and microscopic **bacteria** (plural of **bacterium**), and by various kinds of **fungus**. All the chemical building blocks are dismantled and returned to the soil – and there they are taken up again by the roots of new plants and used to make new stems, leaves, flowers and fruits. If these plants are then eaten, the building blocks may even end up as part of a fly, a fish, a frog or an elephant.

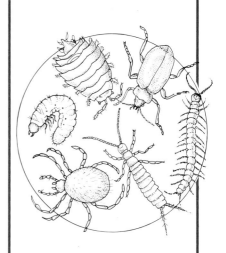

Above: *Without the 'decomposers' the Earth would soon be covered in a thick layer of dead plants and animals. The first stage is often done by beetles, worms and grubs (the **larvae** of flies) but the final breakdown of plant and animal remains is done by fungi and by microscopic bacteria in the soil.*

21

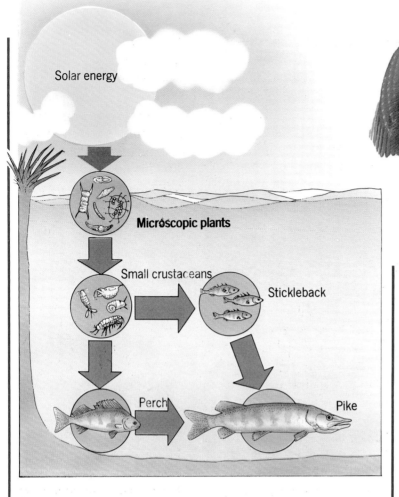

Solar energy

Microscopic plants

Small crustaceans

Stickleback

Perch

Pike

Kingfisher and prey

Food chains and food webs

The grass, the zebra and the lion in the picture on page 21 provide a simple example of what biologists call a **food chain**. It is a way of describing how various animals and plants depend on each other. Another example is shown above. Here, in a freshwater lake or river, microscopic floating plants 'fix' (capture) the Sun's energy. Some are too small to see. Some form the bright green surface slime you often see on a still pond. But they all do exactly the same job as the grasses and trees on land. That is, they make food. It is the first link in the food chain, so the plants are called the producers. Next in line come the primary consumers – the first animals in the 'who-eats-who?' chain – followed by the secondary consumers and finally by the top predator – the hunter at the end of the chain.

The food chain idea is a useful one, but in real life things are more complicated. Most animals eat a variety of different foods, so they play a part in many different chains. The result is that these separate chains become linked together – and this forms a 'food web'.

One of the main threats to nature today comes from industrial chemical waste poured into rivers, and from pesticides washed into rivers from farmland. These poisons can collect in an animal's body fat, and when that animal is eaten, the hunter's body takes in – and keeps – *all*

In the diagram on the left, arrows show how food energy is passed along a typical food chain. Here there are two possible chains – one from plants to crustaceans to perch to pike and the other taking a different route – plants to crustaceans to stickleback to pike. If you imagine a few other common animals of the riverside you can soon see how simple chains can quickly become food webs. The perch, for example, may be eaten by a heron. The stickleback could fall prey to a kingfisher, as it does here. The crustaceans could end up as food for a caddis fly larva and even the top predator, the pike, could be caught by its one enemy – the angler.

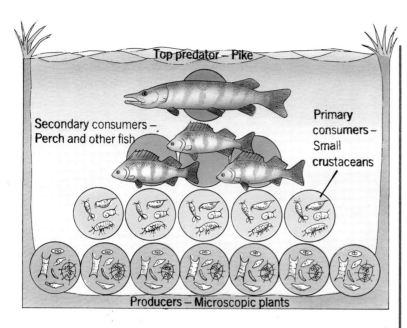

Top predator – Pike

Secondary consumers – Perch and other fish

Primary consumers – Small crustaceans

Producers – Microscopic plants

The food pyramid on the left gives an idea of just how much food it takes to keep a natural system like a pond alive and healthy. Roughly 1000 kilograms of plant life is needed to feed the animals that feed the fish that in turn feed just 1 kilogram of pike.

the poison its victim ever ate. This happens every time the hunter catches an animal with poison in its body, and eventually the hunter is killed. This is why so many owls, eagles and hawks are now endangered species.

The pyramid of life

In every habitat there are always millions upon millions of insects and other tiny creatures, far fewer big, slow, harmless animals, and just a very few big fierce hunters. The reason for this is that only a small amount of the total food energy gets passed along the food chain. Nine-tenths of the food an animal eats is used as fuel – for keeping warm and moving about. Only one-tenth is used for growing and putting on weight, so only that small amount is turned into food for the next animal in the chain.

Below: *Once the lions have made a kill and settled down to feed, the remaining zebras relax and carry on grazing without any sign of alarm. They know that once they have killed, the lions will not attack again.*

A place to live

Just what will grow where on the Earth's surface is controlled mainly by the climate – the annual amount of rain and sunshine and the average temperature.

The different vegetation zones encircle the Earth in broad bands. A traveller starting in dense tropical rainforest near the equator would pass through grasslands and desert regions, then mixed woodlands and dark pine forests, before finally emerging into the cold, barren, treeless plains of the polar **tundra**. These vegetation zones make up the major **habitats** of the Earth. Each one has its own special features and each is home to a group of typical, and often highly specialized, animals.

The polar regions

The north and south polar regions are bitterly cold windswept wildernesses, but in most other ways they are total opposites. The Arctic is a frozen ocean, almost completely surrounded by land. Antarctica is a continent, bigger than Europe and the United States added together, and surrounded by the Southern Ocean.

In the Arctic, most life is found on land. The lichens and mosses and tough grasses that survive there are food for hares and lemmings, birds like the ptarmigan, and herds of musk ox, reindeer and caribou. The main hunters are arctic foxes, snowy owls and falcons. The seas are rich in fish and shellfish that provide food for seals and walruses. The most powerful hunter of all is the polar bear.

Above: *The range of the polar bear extends right around the Arctic region. The bear is mainly a hunter of seals, but will also take walruses, fish, and even sea-birds' eggs.*

Below: *In Africa, the parallel bands of vegetation show quite clearly. In other regions the pattern is distorted by mountains and other natural features.*

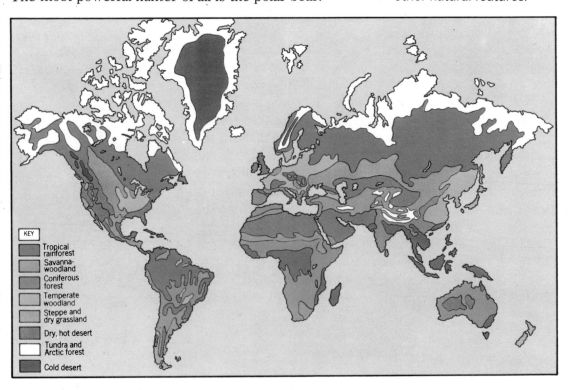

KEY
- Tropical rainforest
- Savanna-woodland
- Coniferous forest
- Temperate woodland
- Steppe and dry grassland
- Dry, hot desert
- Tundra and Arctic forest
- Cold desert

Antarctica has no true land animals. Penguins, skuas and other birds nest there in summer. Seals come out on to the rocky shores to breed. But all return to the sea once the short breeding season is over. Antarctic food chains are all based on life in the sea. Everything starts with the 'phytoplankton' – tiny plants floating in the surface waters. Next in the chain is the 'zooplankton' – masses of minute drifting animals that include the larvae of crabs, starfish, jellyfish and many others, as well as the much larger shrimp-like krill that provide the main source of food for blue whales and other baleen whales.

Grassland, savanna and steppe

There are various types of grassland. Some, like the African savanna, are hot, while others, such as the North American prairie and the steppes of Asia are much colder. We have taken over most of the world's natural grasslands for growing crops or for grazing cattle and sheep.

But natural grasslands, and their animal residents, do survive. Usually they are a mixture of long and short grasses with scattered clumps of low trees and thorn bushes. The most obvious animals of this habitat are the herds of plant-eaters such as the antelopes, zebra and wildebeeste of the savanna. Less obvious, but also very typical, are the burrowing animals – the prairie dogs of North America, the viscachas of South America and the hamsters, marmots and moles of Europe and Asia. While the big plains animals provide food for lions, leopards and cheetahs, the smaller animals are hunted by foxes, eagles, snakes and various members of the weasel family.

In many grasslands the food supply is changed by wet and dry seasons. Food is also thinly spread out in this habitat. For these reasons, the larger grassland animals are constantly on the move, following the rains and searching for fresh pastures.

Above: *Wildebeeste are among the most common savanna grazers. Huge herds migrate across the plains of East Africa, following the rains and the fresh grass they produce.*

Monkey

Giraffe

Elephant

Gerenuk

Eland

Dik-dik

Wart-hog

Above: *Evolution has made sure that Africa's savanna-woodlands support as many animals as possible. By feeding at slightly different levels, the animals share out the food without having to fight each other for it.*

Toucans feeding on fruit

Spider monkeys

Tree snake

Above: *South American monkeys are more primitive than those of Africa and Asia. One distinctive feature is that many can grip with their tails.*

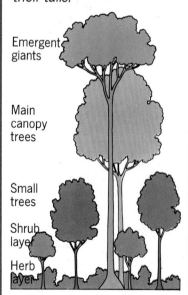

Emergent giants

Main canopy trees

Small trees

Shrub layer

Herb layer

The vegetation in a typical rainforest forms five main horizontal layers or 'strata'. The lower three are often known as the 'understorey'.

Tropical rainforest

The rainforest is a curiously upside-down world. Trees rise straight up for 30 metres or more and then spread out so that their crowns become interwoven to form an almost continuous green 'roof' – the **canopy** – high above the ground. The result is that very little light reaches the ground. It is dark, and dripping wet, with hardly any undergrowth except where a tree has fallen and torn a hole in the canopy, or at the forest edge where light can penetrate the gloom.

In the heart of the forest, most animal life is to be found far above the ground. There are no herds of ground-dwelling grazers like those of the grasslands. Here, the only large forest-floor animals are wild pigs rooting in the earth, and shy 'loners' like the African bongo and okapi, nibbling at the leaves of low-growing shrubs. The true grazers here are the monkeys and sloths, leaf-eating insects and countless seed- and fruit-eating birds. The hunters, too, have taken to the trees. In addition to powerful eagles there are lizards and snakes, tree-climbing anteaters and several members of the cat family.

Because there are hardly any seasonal changes at all in the tropical forests, flowers and fruits appear all year round. There is a constant wealth of food, and so these forests are the richest wildlife habitats on Earth.

Seasonal woodlands

The woodlands of the temperate regions support a great variety of animal life – but these animals have had to adapt their life-styles to the seasonal changes that take place every year. In the summer months the trees themselves, the shrub layer of brambles and other bushes, and the ground layer of grasses, wild flowers and mosses, provide a rich harvest of food. There are leaves, nuts and berries for the plant-eaters and plenty of insects and grubs, mice and voles for the meat-eaters. For a few months there is more than enough for everyone. But all that changes in the autumn. The leaves fall, the clouds of insects are gone, and the woodland residents change to their winter behaviour. Many of the birds **migrate** to warmer lands and do not return until the following spring. Animals such as squirrels and field-mice lay down stores of food for the winter, while hedgehogs, dormice and most woodland bats, **hibernate** through the cold winter months.

Deserts

The desert lands are the most harsh and difficult of all the Earth's habitats. The main problem, of course, is the shortage of water, and many desert animals are specialized so that they do not need to drink. Instead, they obtain all the water they need from the seeds or insects they eat. Larger animals must stay within range of a water hole or stream, although some birds fly enormous distances every day, to and from watering places.

Most desert animals also conserve their body moisture as much as possible. Many of them do not sweat, and most pass only small amounts of very concentrated urine. Above all, they avoid the full glare of the sun. Hunters and hunted alike tend to be most active at night, or at dawn and dusk: most take to the shade of rocks or vegetation, or disappear into burrows, in the heat of the day.

Below: *While the squirrel survives the winter on stored food, and the hedgehog hibernates, the crossbill's specialized bill enables it to feed on the one kind of seed that is available in winter – spruce, larch and fir cones.*

Hedgehog

Squirrel

Crossbill

Below: *Very few deserts are completely without plants. Here, in the typical red-rock desert of Australia, the vast desert plain has a thin covering of coarse grass and dry bushes.*

2. The Plant Kingdom

More than 375,000 different plant species have so far been studied and officially named by scientists. Many are extremely common, others are very rare indeed and are sometimes known only from a few ancient museum specimens. But these are just the ones we know about. In the world's unexplored jungles and remote mountain regions there could be almost as many again – still waiting to be discovered and studied.

As well as being the most ancient form of life on Earth, plants are without any doubt the great record-breakers of the natural world. Firstly, they are by far the largest living things the world has ever seen. Many specimens of Douglas fir and giant redwood in the west coast mountain forests of America tower more than 110 metres into the sky, and the heaviest specimen of all has been estimated to weigh in at more than 6000 tonnes – 32 times as heavy as the biggest blue whale ever recorded.

Secondly, plants are the longest-living things on Earth. Some kinds of shellfish (clams) live for 200 years. Human beings very rarely pass 110 years. And yet in the plant world, ages measured in hundreds of years are commonplace, and the oldest plants are known to live for thousands. Some of the lichens found in Antarctica are more than 10,000 years old. They started growing when the people of northern Europe were primitive hunters, dressed in animal skins and armed with spears and bows. Closer to home, one of the gnarled and twisted bristlecone pines in the desert of Arizona has been dated at 4600 years old, a mere youngster by comparison with Antarctica's lichens, yet it sprouted from seed at about the time the Great Pyramid of King Cheops was built in ancient Egypt.

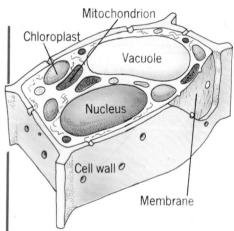

Above: *A typical plant cell is roughly rectangular and has a very tough outer wall made of cellulose strands, with a thin flexible inner lining called the cell membrane.*

The liquid inside the cell is a weak solution of salts and sugars, and floating in it are several specialized structures. The nucleus *is the cell's control centre, the* chloroplasts *manufacture sugars and starches, and the* mitochondria *are chemical power-houses that enable the plant to use its stored food.*

Above: *The sundew is one of several plants that catch and digest insects to obtain the nitrogen they require.*

Right: *This 'family tree' shows the main divisions used by botanists to classify the plant kingdom. Because they are so different from other plants, fungi (plural of fungus) and bacteria are sometimes given completely separate kingdoms.*

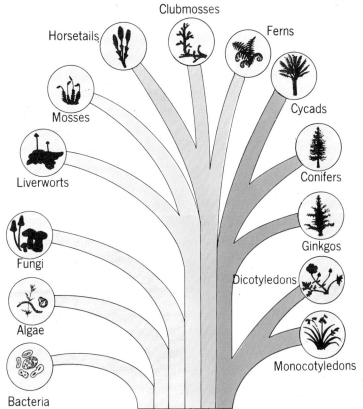

Clubmosses

Horsetails

Ferns

Mosses

Cycads

Liverworts

Conifers

Fungi

Ginkgos

Dicotyledons

Algae

Monocotyledons

Bacteria

29

Seaweeds and their relatives

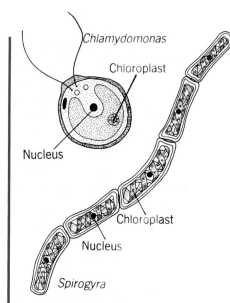

Chlamydomonas

Chloroplast

Nucleus

Chloroplast

Nucleus

Spirogyra

Algae (plural of alga) are the simplest and most primitive of all plants on Earth. They have no roots, no flowers or seeds – yet they come in an enormous variety of shapes and sizes.

Most of the algae are water plants, although a few do live on land in damp places. One of the most common land algae is a single-celled plant called *Pleurococcus* which forms a pale green powdery growth on trees and fences.

The simplest of the water algae are also single-celled plants. Many are far too small to be seen with the naked eye, but they are very important because they are the first stage in the aquatic food chain. Without such tiny plants as the pond alga *Chlamydomonas*, illustrated here, many ponds and lakes would be unable to support any animal life. Another very common water alga is *Spirogyra*, which forms long threads of cells joined end to end. This is the plant that often forms a bright green surface slime on still ponds and drainage ditches. Under a microscope each cell can be seen to contain a coiled-up spiral ribbon bearing the food-producing **chloroplasts**, and a dark central spot which is the **nucleus** of the cell.

Above: Chlamydomonas *re-produces either by simply dividing to produce as many as 32 new cells, or by pro-ducing quite separate male and female cells which join together to make a com-pletely new plant.*

Spirogyra *is also able to reproduce by both sexual and non-sexual methods.*

SEAWEEDS

Different seaweeds grow on different parts of the beach. Some are always found at the top of the beach near the high-tide line. Others grow only in deep water beyond the low-water line, where they are never ex-posed to the air.

These shoreline plants provide a safe home for many animals. Lift up a mass of soggy weed and you will find crabs and lim-pets, anemones and sand-hoppers. The weed prevents them from being dried out by the sun and wind, and also protects them from hungry gulls and shorebirds.

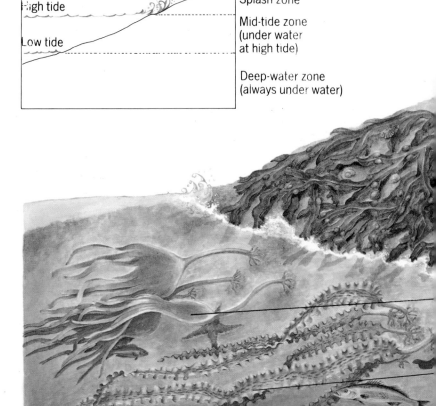

High tide

Low tide

Splash zone

Mid-tide zone
(under water
at high tide)

Deep-water zone
(always under water)

Pleurococcus reproduces by making **spores**, which are carried away by the wind and start to grow wherever they land. Many water algae also produce spores, but others reproduce sexually. Male cells are released into the water and these can swim, using whip-like tails, until they meet the female egg cells of another plant. The two then join and grow into a new plant.

At the opposite end of the size scale are the giants of the algae family – enormous seaweeds such as the giant kelp, which grows up to 60 metres in length. The most familiar members of the family are the green and brown seaweeds found on rocky shores. Look closely at some of these plants and you can see how evolution has equipped them to survive the constant pounding of the waves and the repeated soaking and drying out as the tides surge in and out. Many have a branching foot or 'holdfast' to anchor them to the rocks. The stem is tough and elastic so that it can swish around in the waves without breaking. The main blade is usually broad and flat so that it can soak up as much energy as possible from the Sun. Many species also have small air-filled floats or 'bladders' to keep them up in the sunlit surface waters.

In some parts of the world seaweeds are collected as food. In others they are used to make fertilizer. But today they are most important as a source of chemicals called alginates – used in hundreds of everyday products.

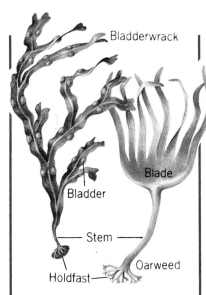

The bladderwrack and oarweed, pictured above, show many of the main features of the seaweeds of rocky shores.

The holdfast produces an adhesive which glues the plant to the rock, while a jelly-like coating helps stop the plants being dried out in hot dry weather.

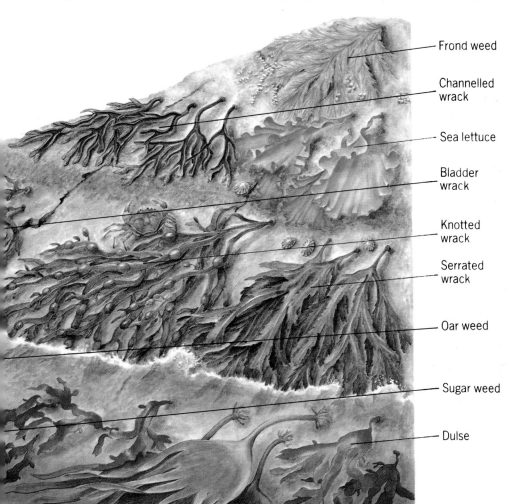

- Frond weed
- Channelled wrack
- Sea lettuce
- Bladder wrack
- Knotted wrack
- Serrated wrack
- Oar weed
- Sugar weed
- Dulse

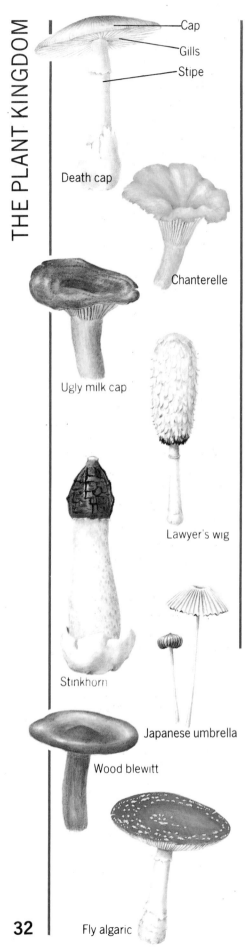

Cap
Gills
Stipe

Death cap

Chanterelle

Ugly milk cap

Lawyer's wig

Stinkhorn

Japanese umbrella

Wood blewitt

Fly algaric

Fungi – the villains of the plant world

The fungi (plural of fungus) do not really qualify to be called plants at all, because unlike the true plants, they contain none of the green chemical chlorophyll and therefore they cannot make their own supplies of food. Instead, they are the robbers, thieves and bandits of the plant world. What they cannot make themselves they have to take from other, normal, green plants – or salvage from the leaves, twigs and other remains that end up lying on the ground.

Unlike the cells of a normal plant, the cells of a fungus are not surrounded by a wall of cellulose. Instead, their walls are made of a material called chitin – the same substance that forms the horny outer covering of shrimps and many kinds of insect. Because its own cell walls are not made of cellulose, the fungus is able to produce special chemicals called enzymes which break down cellulose – and this enables the fungus to feed on the cells and cell contents of other plants.

It is this special chemistry that makes the fungi so useful for some things – and such a terrible nuisance, and danger, at the same time. Fungi are useful first of all because, along with bacteria, they carry out the very important job of breaking down and recycling the remains of dead animals and plants. They are the great waste-disposal specialists of the natural world. They are also useful in our food and drinks industries. The yeasts we use to bake our bread and to make wines and beers are all fungi. Other kinds of fungus produce some of our most useful medicines – such as penicillin.

The problem with fungi is that they will grow on, and ruin, anything made of cellulose. Moulds and mildews spoil

Mushrooms and toadstools have been used for hundreds of years in recipes and in traditional medicines. But great care is needed. Some are extremely good to eat; others are deadly!

Mushrooms and toadstools come in a great variety of shapes and sizes. The 'Death cap' at the top of the page shows the main parts of the 'fruiting body' of a typical mushroom or toadstool.

Above: *The American giant puff-ball is the largest known fruiting body. It grows to more than 1.5 metres diameter.*

stored food, clothing, furniture, books – anything made of wood, wood-pulp, cotton or any other plant material that has become damp enough for their spores to germinate. This is because all these things are made of cells with cellulose walls. Fungi also cause diseases in crops such as potatoes and maize and also in animals, including people.

Fungi reproduce by releasing clouds of minute spores which drift on the wind. If they land in a suitable cool damp place, where food is available, they start to grow – sending out masses of fine white threads that look rather like cotton wool. This woolly mass is the fungus plant and is called the 'mycelium'. When the fungus is ready to reproduce again it has to make special arrangements to release its spores – especially as many fungi live underground, or inside rotten wood or fruit, well away from the open air. In some species tiny capsules containing the spores are raised up on the ends of tall threads. At the right moment the capsules explode, scattering the spores in all directions. Other kinds of fungus develop the large and often colourful structures we call mushrooms and toadstools. The spores are produced in the grooves beneath the mushroom's cap and are released into the breeze when ripe. Many fungi spend their entire lives in the soil or inside other plants, spreading their threads far and wide and frequently killing the plants they live on. Often, the only time these fungi are seen is when they send their special 'fruiting bodies' to the surface to release a new batch of spores.

Above: *The honey fungus is an attractive woodland species – but it is a killer. Beneath its 'pie crust' fruiting bodies, masses of thread-like mycelium take over the tree and kill it.*

Below: *Mould spores are always present in the air, and uncovered food offers a perfect place to grow.*

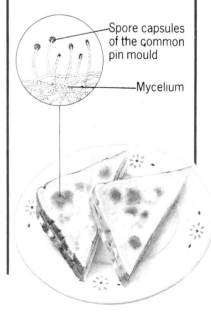

Spore capsules of the common pin mould

Mycelium

Lichens and mosses

The most familiar kinds of lichen are probably the small round crusty patches of green, grey and orange that grow on old stone walls and exposed rocks. But there are others too. Some are branched or leaf-like in appearance, and grow over the trunks and branches of woodland trees. Others have green upright stems with bright red tips. Some – such as 'old man's beard' – festoon themselves from the branches of trees, while one of the largest kinds, known as 'reindeer moss', carpets large areas of ground in the frozen Arctic regions. (It really *is* a lichen, not a moss, but it is the main food of the reindeer herds.)

The fascinating thing about lichens is that each one is not just a single plant but a living partnership of two completely different plants – a fungus and an alga. Most of the lichen consists of a mass of fungal threads, but embedded in this mass are numerous algal cells. The partnership is a complex one, but it seems that the fungus obtains food (sugars) from the alga (which of course contains chlorophyll) while the alga gets a good supply of water and mineral nutrients from the surrounding fungus.

Most of these fungi and algae can live separately, but together they are a remarkable team. They can live in a wide range of habitats – from Antarctica to the hottest desert, on mountain tops and rocky sea-shores. They can

Below: *A cross-section through a crusty lichen is rather like a section of a pie.*

The top and bottom are made of fungal threads that are packed tightly together into a dense mat. Inside, the lichen consists of much looser threads, and large green photosynthetic algal cells that produce all the partnership's food supplies.

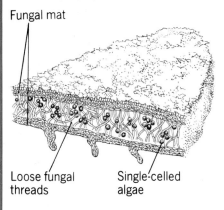

Fungal mat

Loose fungal threads

Single-celled algae

Lichens come in many sizes, shapes and colours. The crusty brown lichen (left) is common on walls and roof slates. The reindeer 'moss' (below) is a common lichen of the Arctic tundra zone.

withstand being completely dried out for long periods of time. And they live for thousands of years. At least they do in clean air. Unfortunately, lichens are very sensitive to air pollution, especially to sulphur dioxide fumes, and they have almost vanished from some industrial areas.

Mosses and liverworts

Mosses and their close relatives the liverworts are primitive plants that grow in dense cushion-like masses on damp ground. They have no true roots, and the water and nutrients they absorb from their wet habitat simply pass through the plant from cell to cell. There are no special water-carrying tubes like those found in trees and other advanced plants.

Mosses were one of the earliest plant groups to leave the oceans and live on land. But still they remain tied to the water. Without it they cannot reproduce. The reason for this is that the plants produce separate male and female reproductive cells – and the male cells, or **sperm**, have to make their way to the egg cells in order to fertilize them. They do this by swimming, by means of a whip-like tail, but they can do this only if the surface of the leaf is covered by a film of water.

Above: *Sphagnum moss is a typical moss of boggy areas. Its special cells hold water like a sponge.*

Below: *The main parts of a mature moss plant.*

Capsule

Stalk

Simple leaves

Rhizoids

35

Clubmosses, horsetails and ferns

Clubmosses, horsetails and ferns are another very ancient group of plants, and they show many of the important changes that plants had to make when they left the safety of the seas and started to live on land.

Seaweeds and water-weeds usually collapse in a soggy heap when they are taken from the water. This is because they do not need stiff stems. The water usually supports their weight. So – the first thing the early land plants needed was a proper stem to support them and hold their leaves up to the light so that photosynthesis could take place efficiently. They also needed roots – to anchor them in the ground and to collect water and minerals from the soil. But with their water supply beneath the ground and their leaves perhaps many metres up in the air, the new land plants also needed a proper system of pipes to carry liquids from one part of the plant to another.

All these new developments can be seen in the members of the fern family, even in fossils more than 300 million years old. And 300 million years ago was the hey-day of these plants. The great swamp forests of the Carboniferous period consisted of giant clubmosses and horsetails that would dwarf their modern relatives.

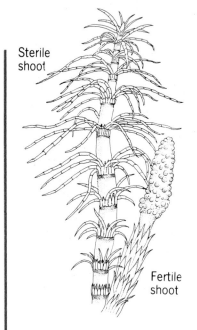

Sterile shoot

Fertile shoot

The upright stem of the horsetail Equisetum *above bears rings of branches that are sterile – they cannot reproduce. The fertile spore-bearing stems are smaller and less easy to find.*

The present day Equisetum *is about 1.5m tall. Its ancestor* Calamites *grew to 20m!*

Giant horsetails and club-mosses dominated the swamp forests of 300 million years ago. They left many fossils, like the Cala-mites *leaf (1) and* Lepido-dendron *stem (2) below.*

Lepidodendron

Horsetail

Hylonomus

Right: *Modern tree-ferns in the New Zealand rainforest.* Below: *A fern's life starts when small packages of spores (sori) grow on the undersides of the leaf fronds (1). The spores are released and are carried away by the wind. Where they land, a 'prothallus' grows (2). This produces both sperm cells and egg cells. The final stage is the growth of a new fern (3).*

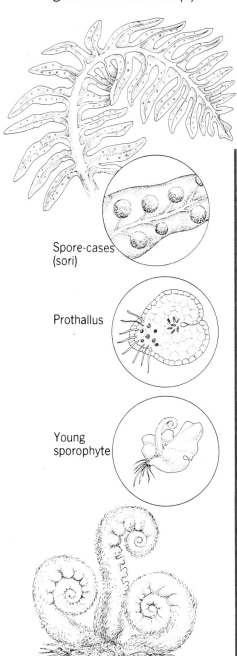

Spore-cases (sori)

Prothallus

Young sporophyte

As these huge forest plants died and fell, their woody remains built up, layer upon layer, but they did not rot away completely. Instead, they became buried under thick layers of mud and sand. For millions of years they were crushed and squeezed under the weight of the rocks above them, until finally they too became rock – a very special and useful kind of rock, called coal.

The ferns are by far the most successful members of this large plant family, and they are also much more varied than their relatives. Some are small water plants. Others, such as bracken, grow in woodland and on hillsides. But largest of all are the tropical tree-ferns, some of which grow up to 25 metres tall.

Like most of their relatives, ferns have a two-stage life-cycle. For the main part of its life a fern is the familiar leafy bracken-like plant, with a tough stem and large fronds that uncurl in the spring. But this is only part of the story. This plant is called the 'sporophyte', and it produces spores which are held in small orange or brown spore-cases on the underside of the leaf-fronds. The spores are then released into the air, and when they land on damp ground they start to grow. But instead of a familiar fern plant, what appears next is a tiny heart-shaped plant just over two centimetres across. This too is a fern. It is called the 'gametophyte' plant, and in this part of its life-cycle it produces male sperm cells and female egg cells. If the leaves are wet, so that the sperm cells can swim, then one of the eggs will be fertilized and a new sporophyte plant will start to grow.

37

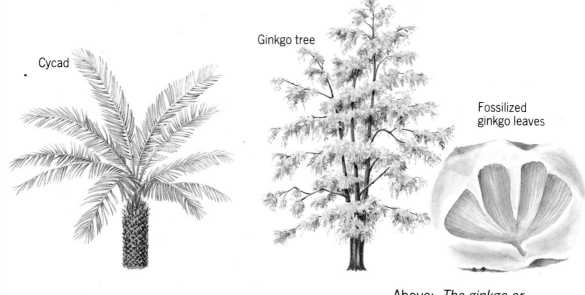

Cycad

Ginkgo tree

Fossilized ginkgo leaves

Welwitschia

Above: *The ginkgo or maidenhair tree has not changed for 150 million years. We know this from fossilized leaves. The cycad and* Welwitschia *are other ancient gymnosperms. The male parts of the desert plant* Welwitschia *look more like flowers than cones.*

The seed plants

The cone-bearing plants, illustrated opposite, and the flowering plants on the next two pages, together make up a large and very important plant group that is called the seed plants.

Producing **seeds** was a huge improvement on the earlier methods of reproduction because it finally enabled these plants to break free from watery habitats. Instead of relying on delicate swimming sperms to carry the male cells to the waiting female cells, they developed a system of dry **pollen** grains to do the same job. The pollen could be transported in many different ways (see page 49) and this enabled the plants to take over many new habitats. They moved up the mountains and out into the deserts, clothing the surface of the Earth with thousands of completely new plant species.

The cone-bearers
The conifers and their relatives all bear cones, usually small pollen-bearing male cones and larger seed-bearing female cones. Their botanical name is the 'gymnosperms', which means 'naked seed' and they get this name from the

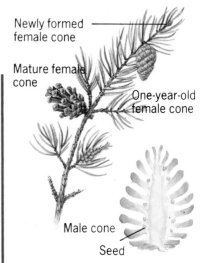

Newly formed female cone

Mature female cone

One-year-old female cone

Male cone

Seed

The Scots pine twig above shows the small male cone and the much larger female cones. It is usually possible to find female cones of different ages on the same twig. The smaller drawing shows the position of the 'naked' seeds inside the cone.

Norway spruce

Cedar of Lebanon

Scots pine

Coast redwood

European larch

Coniferous trees grow very quickly compared with most deciduous trees, and their shapes are also very characteristic. The drawing above shows some of the main conifer species of Europe and North America, with illustrations of their mature female cones.

fact that the seeds themselves sit openly on the surface of the woody plates that make up the female cone.

The cycads are a primitive group of cone-bearing plants which had their hey-day between 100 and 150 million years ago. Today there are about 100 species, growing mainly in the tropical regions. Most of them look rather like palms, with thick, medium-height stems and large fern-like leaves. Some have cones as big as footballs.

The main group consists of the modern conifers – the firs, pines and spruces that make up the great temperate and northern forests of the world. They are nearly all evergreen trees. Instead of shedding all their leaves in autumn they keep them for up to ten years, constantly shedding and replacing them a few at a time. The leaves are thin and needle-shaped, with a tough waxy coating. Both are special adaptations to enable them to function even in the cold winter months. Because they are better equipped for cold and dry regions, the conifers grow higher up on mountains and much nearer the polar regions than the much more sensitive **deciduous** trees.

Conifers grow quickly and evenly, with tall straight stems and few side branches, and for this reason they are our main source of building timber, floor-boards and wood for making furniture. The wood is also turned into pulp for making paper, card and hardboard.

39

The flowering plants

Of all the plants known to science, more than 250,000 are flowering plants. They are by far the most varied and adaptable and successful plants on Earth, and they come in an astonishing range of shapes and sizes.

This enormous division of the plant kingdom includes all the grasses, rushes and reeds – more than 10,000 different species. These range from the wheat, maize, barley, oats and rice that feed most of the world's people, to the grazing grasses that feed our cows and sheep and the giant bamboos of Asia which grow so big that they are used instead of wood for building houses and bridges.

This group also includes 'succulent' plants (ones that can store moisture) such as cacti that grow in the desert and semi-desert regions of the world. It includes the flowering trees of forests, woods and orchards – everything from sycamore, beech, apple and plum to the teak and mahogany, coffee and rubber trees of tropical regions. It includes peas and beans, potatoes and cabbage, climbing vines and spices and herbs. And last but not least it includes the hundreds of plants we value for their beauty alone – the roses, daffodils, orchids and lilies, plants from every habitat on Earth, from mountains and moors to marshes and woods.

The one characteristic that is shared by every one of

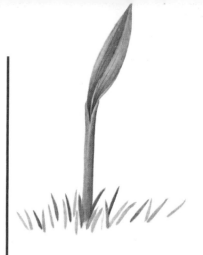

Above: *Monocotyledon seedlings have just one seed-leaf. At first, as it pushes up through the soil, the leaf is protected by a tough outer sheath. But as soon as it breaks the surface, the leaf turns green and starts to photosynthesize. Most of the 'monocots' are herbs and grasses; only the palms grow to tree size.*

Below: *A selection of monocotyledon plants.*

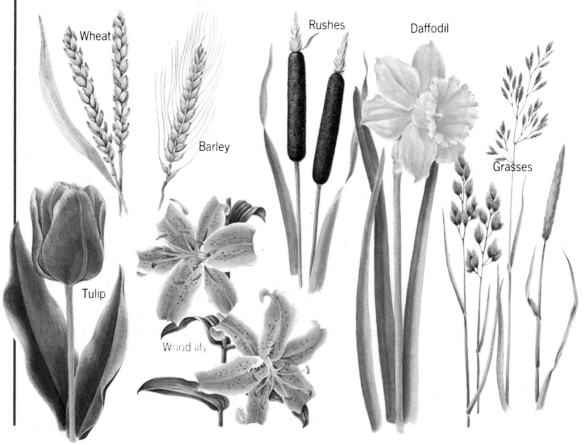

Wheat

Barley

Rushes

Daffodil

Grasses

Tulip

Wood lily

Above: *Dicotyledon seedlings have a pair of seed-leaves, and in many species, such as the peas and beans, these are swollen into a food store. Instead of pushing straight up through the soil, many dicot seedlings have a hooked tip that protects the young leaves.*
Unlike the 'monocots', many 'dicots' have tough woody stems.
Below: *A selection of dicotyledon plants.*

these plants is that they all produce flowers. Some are large and colourful. Some are so tiny they can be seen only with a magnifying lens. But they are all built to a similar basic design and they all have just one essential job to do. That job is to make sure that pollen of exactly the right type reaches the egg cells so that seeds can be produced, and to provide a container for those seeds. And that is the important difference between the flowering plants – the 'angiosperms' – and the other seed plants called gymnosperms. Angiosperm means 'enclosed seed', and all the plants in this group enclose their seeds in a special container called an 'ovary'.

The large illustrations below show typical members of the two main sub-groups of the flowering plants – the **monocotyledons** and the **dicotyledons**. Cotyledons are the very first leaves to appear when a seed germinates – that is, when it splits open and starts to grow (see page 52). In some plants – monocotyledons – there is just one of these seed-leaves. Most plants in this group have long narrow leaves with parallel veins, and their flower petals and sepals are arranged in threes. The dicotyledons have two seed-leaves, and their leaves usually have a branching network of veins. The flowers of dicotyledons have their petals and sepals arranged in groups of four, five or more.

The flowering plants are the most advanced and highly developed members of the plant kingdom and so the next chapter concentrates on how they work.

Black-eyed Susan

Deadnettle

Poppy

Pear tree

Rose

Potato

Broad bean

3. Plants in Action

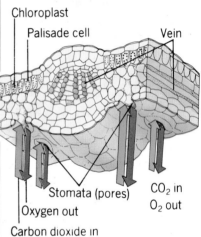

Chloroplast

Palisade cell

Vein

Stomata (pores)

CO_2 in
O_2 out

Oxygen out

Carbon dioxide in

Above: *In most plants, photosynthesis is concentrated in the tall 'palisade' cells in the upper part of the leaf. Water and nutrients are carried to the food-producing cells by a network of veins, while gases pass in and out of the leaf by tiny pores called 'stomata'.*

Left: *An oak tree, just starting out in life – as a very young sapling.*

What can plants do?

The closer we look into the world of plants, the more surprising and fascinating it becomes. It is all too easy to think that plants simply sit there and grow. But their private lives are far more complicated than appears at first sight. They feed and breathe. Some have plumbing systems that can pump thousands of litres of water a day from beneath the ground to heights of up to 100 metres. They can tell the time, and the season of the year. Some can count, and remember things as well. They know which way up they are, and can turn their faces to follow the Sun. Some catch insects. Others use birds, bees, bats and other animals to transport their pollen and to spread their seeds far and wide. All of which is not bad for things that 'just sit there and grow'.

The living food factory

Living things are just like engines. They need fuel if they are to continue working. Animals take in their fuel in the form of food – by eating plants or by eating other animals that eat plants. They then 'burn' this fuel using the oxygen they take in from the air. The important thing to remember is that no animal can actually *make* food. Only plants can do that – and the process takes place actually inside their leaves.

The leaf is the plant's food factory, and the main food-producing machines are the tiny green particles called **chloroplasts** that give the leaves (and some other parts of the plant) their characteristic colour. Here, the plant carries out the 'green magic' of **photosynthesis** – the chemical process that supports all living things. The raw materials needed for photosynthesis are water (and tiny amounts of dissolved minerals) piped up to the leaf from the roots down below, carbon dioxide gas which the plant takes in through tiny holes, mainly in the underside of the leaf, and the energy in the rays of the Sun. Inside the green photosynthetic cells the carbon and oxygen and hydrogen from these raw materials are used to build sugars, the main food-fuel, and starches, which are used as a means of storing energy. These chemical processes do not use up all the oxygen that is available, and the 'spare' oxygen is released through the holes in the leaves – constantly 'topping up' and freshening the oxygen supply in the Earth's atmosphere.

Some of the sugars produced by a plant are used straight away to fuel its own life-support systems. Others are combined in various ways to make starch as a winter food store, or cellulose for new cell walls. Some sugars are also used to make the small amounts of oils, resins, fats, colourings and other specialized chemicals that the plant needs during its life.

Water is drawn up the stem of a plant by suction, caused by water evaporating into the air from the surfaces of the leaves.

You can see how much water is lost in this way by enclosing a large leaf in a clear plastic bag on a warm day. Within a few hours the inside of the bag will be misty with water droplets.

In warm dry weather, plants lose water from their leaves by evaporation faster than they can draw it in through their roots. The packing cells lose their hydraulic pressure and the plant wilts.

Clear water   Water dyed
with ink

Above: *By splitting a carna-
tion stem like this, you can
show that water is carried
up the stem in separate
tubes rather than just being
soaked up by the whole
stem like water rising up
through a sponge.*

*Half the flower will turn
blue, the other half will
remain white.*

Plant stems, roots and plumbing systems

The cells in a typical plant stem are arranged in a very
precise way, and the various different types of cells have a
variety of different jobs to do.

The outermost layer is called the 'epidermis', and it
consists of a single layer of very tough cells with a waxy,
waterproof outer coating. These cells help the stem keep
its shape, and also help prevent water loss through the
stem walls. The 'cortex' and 'pith' cells are mainly large,
unspecialized cells whose main job is to provide the
packing and strength of the stem. In a healthy plant they
are pumped full of water under pressure so that they press
hard against each other and against the epidermis. In this
way they keep the stem rigid. In some plants the outer
layers of the cortex contain cells with chloroplasts. Such
plants have green stems which produce a certain amount
of food and store it in the form of starch grains.

Between the cortex and the pith lies a ring of very
specialized structures called 'vascular bundles'. The name
simply means 'bundles of tubes' and it is these tubes that
provide the main plumbing system of the plant. The inner
part of each bundle consists of thick-walled tubes called
'xylem' (pronounced *zylem*). These carry water up the

*In dicotyledons, shown on
the right, the vascular bundles are arranged in a neat
ring. More tubes, plus tough
woody strengthen-
ing cells, are added each
year, and the stem gets
thicker as well as taller. You
can see this effect on old
climbing roses.*

*In monocotyledons, such
as grasses, palms and
flowers of the lily family, the
bundles of xylem and
phloem are scattered
throughout the stem. As the
plant gets older, the stem
lengthens but does not get
any thicker.*

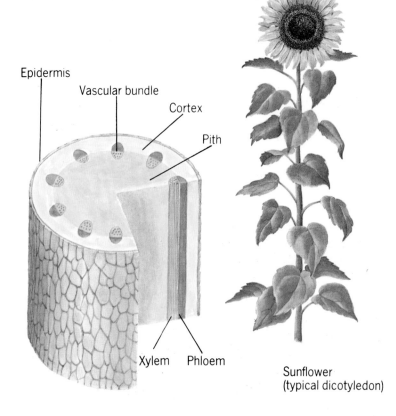

Epidermis

Vascular bundle

Cortex

Pith

Xylem   Phloem

Sunflower
(typical dicotyledon)

stem from the roots. The outer part consists of thin-walled tubes called 'phloem' (*flow-em*) and these carry the food made in the leaves to other parts of the plant – either for immediate use or for storage.

In woody plants such as trees the arrangement is rather different because such enormous plants need much more plumbing to keep them functioning properly. They also need much more strengthening to hold them up. To provide all this the tree has much more xylem and phloem, and the two systems form complete rings around the stem rather than small separate bundles. Also, as the tree gets bigger the old xylem in the centre dies and hardens into what we then call wood. This tough central pillar supports the tree – and provides one of nature's most useful and versatile materials.

Above: *Wood is a very valuable material. Once trees have been cut down, the logs (trunks) are often floated down river to a saw mill. There they are cut up for various uses.*

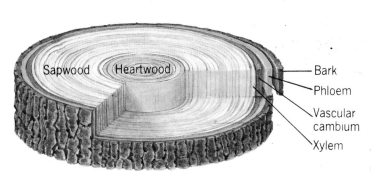

Above: *In a tree stem, the vascular bundles spread out sideways until they meet to form two continuous rings – one of xylem and one of phloem. Between the phloem and xylem there is a special layer, just one cell thick, called the vascular cambium. Here, the living cells are continuously dividing to produce new phloem tubes on the outside, and new xylem tubes on the inside.*

One ring of xylem or phloem represents one year's growth, so a tree can be aged by counting its 'annual rings'.

Horse chestnut (typical hardwood tree)

The plant's underground system

Hidden beneath the ground, the roots of a plant form a living system of pipes, filters, store-rooms and chemical factories just as important (and often just as big) as the network of stems, branches and leaves above ground.

Some plants have a large central root called a 'tap-root' which grows almost straight down. Others have many large roots that spread out just beneath the surface of the soil. These main roots are the beginning of a huge network of roots and rootlets that spread out through the soil, anchoring the plant, providing it with water and minerals, and in some cases acting as a food-store.

Near the tip of each root is a region covered in thousands of very fine root hairs, each made of a single cell, and it is this mass of minute hairs that makes the plant so efficient. A single rye plant, for example, may have well over 500 *kilometres* of roots when all the root hairs are taken into account! The cells of the roots are also highly specialized. Between the root hairs and the inner xylem tubes that carry away the water and nutrients there is a very special layer. This acts as a chemical selector – so specialized that it can allow in the chemicals the plant needs, and at the same time keep out those that the plant does not want.

Once inside the root we find the two main plumbing systems. The xylem is there to carry water and nutrients to the leaves far above, while the phloem carries supplies of fuel – sugars from the leaves – to enable the roots to grow and force their way through the ground.

Above: *A mass of tree roots revealed in a river-bank worn away by rushing water.*

The main parts of a root are shown below. Beyond the root-hair zone the root tip is growing fast and forcing its way through the soil. It is protected from damage by a smooth hard root cap.

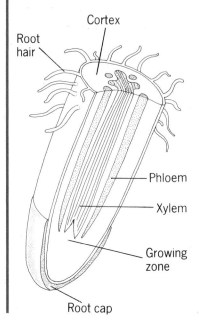

Cortex
Root hair
Phloem
Xylem
Growing zone
Root cap

NEW PLANTS FOR OLD

All flowering plants can reproduce by making seeds. That, after all, is what their flowers are for. But many can also reproduce by a process that does not produce seeds. It is called 'vegetative reproduction'.

Couch grass, for example, can send up new shoots from long underground stems called **rhizomes**. Strawberries make new plants from **runners** – long stems that spread over the soil surface. Every so often they take root and grow into new plants.

Other plants reproduce from underground stems, roots or leaves that have been modified to store food for the winter. Potatoes are swollen storage stems called **tubers**, daffodil **bulbs** are modified leaves, and crocus **corms** are yet another special kind of storage stem.

Some plants, including the house leek can produce tiny new plants on their stems or leaves. These simply drop off when ready and take root in the soil.

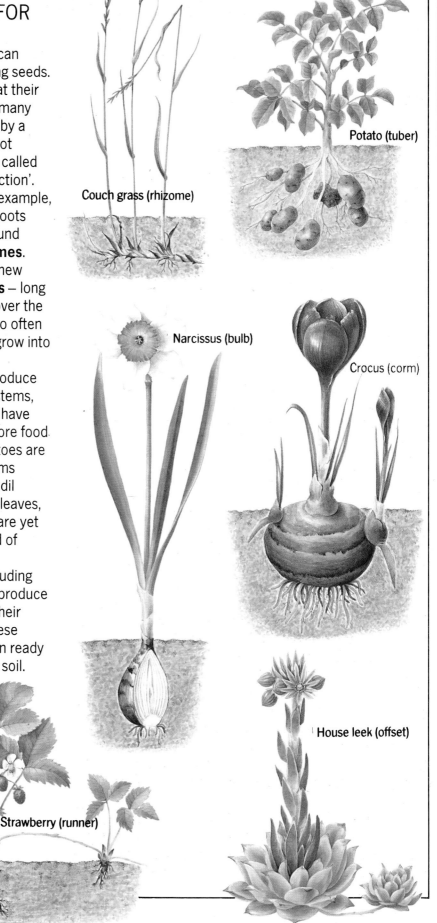

Couch grass (rhizome)

Potato (tuber)

Narcissus (bulb)

Crocus (corm)

Strawberry (runner)

House leek (offset)

Honeysuckle

Rye grass

Thistle

Bee orchid

Buttercup

What is a flower?

The flower is a very special invention of the plant kingdom and it has two essential jobs to do. Its first task is to produce the male and female reproductive cells of the plant – the pollen and egg cells – and provide a way for its own eggs to be fertilized by pollen from another plant. Its second task is to provide a container to protect the egg cells as they develop into seeds. The container is called the **ovary**, and the eggs are called **ovules**. After fertilization, the ovary develops into a **fruit**.

Although flowers look very complicated, and come in hundreds of shapes and sizes, they are all variations on a simple basic design. They are all made from four rings of specially modified leaves at the end of a short stalk. The first, or outer, ring consists of small leaves called 'sepals'. They are usually green and they protect the flower when it first forms as a bud. The next ring consists of petals – often large and brightly coloured. The third ring forms the male sexual parts of the plant – the 'stamens'. These consist of slender stalks with swollen 'anthers' on their tops. The anthers produce the pollen grains, and when they are ripe they split open and release the bright yellow pollen. Right at the centre are the female parts of the plant, but these are sometimes partly hidden. The main part is a thick stalk called the 'style', and this has a sticky and often coloured end called the 'stigma'. This is the 'target' for the pollen grains. If the flower is to be fertilized, pollen grains must

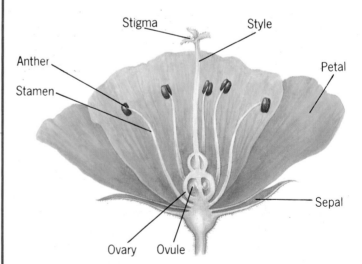

Stigma · Style · Anther · Stamen · Petal · Sepal · Ovary · Ovule

Above: *Despite their very different shapes, all these flowers are variations on a single basic design – four rings of modified leaves on the end of a short stalk.*

Above: *A cross-section through a typical flower shows the layout of the four rings of specialized leaves that form the sepals, petals, stamens and central style.*

The ovary in this example contains several ovules. A cup-shaped flower like this could be pollinated by many different kinds of fly, bee or beetle.

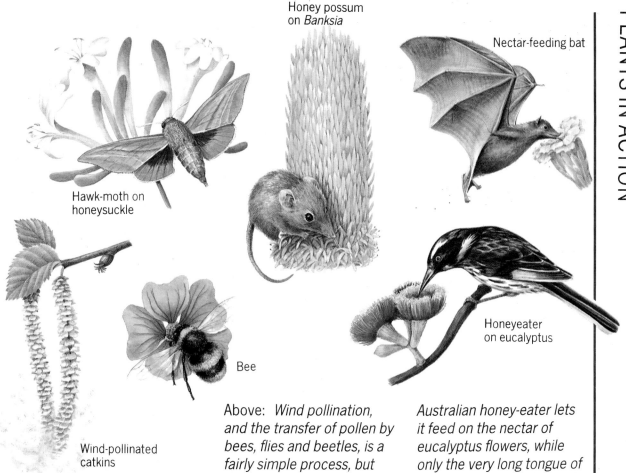

Honey possum
on *Banksia*

Nectar-feeding bat

Hawk-moth on
honeysuckle

Wind-pollinated
catkins

Bee

Honeyeater
on eucalyptus

Above: *Wind pollination, and the transfer of pollen by bees, flies and beetles, is a fairly simple process, but some partnerships need specialized equipment. The long curved bill of an* *Australian honey-eater lets it feed on the nectar of eucalyptus flowers, while only the very long tongue of the hawk-moth could reach right inside honeysuckle flowers.*

land on the stigma. At the lower end of the style, often hidden from view, is the ovary – the container that encloses and protects the ovules, or egg cells. In some flowers there is just one ovule in the ovary; in others there are many ovules.

How does it work?

The first thing a flower has to do is to arrange for its own pollen to be spread to other flowers of its own kind, and at the same time arrange to receive pollen so that its own ovules will be fertilized.

The bright colours, conspicuous shapes and sweet scents of many flowers are not there by chance, or to please human beings. They are special adaptations de-signed to make the flowers attractive to insects, birds and other small animals. As it forces its head inside the flower to get at the sweet nectar inside (the nectar is always right at the bottom, of course) the animal helper is forced to push past the pollen-coated anthers. The result is that its hairs, fur or feathers soon become dusted with the yellow grains. When the animal visits another flower, some of this

Above: *This photograph was taken with film sensitive to ultra-violet light. The lines radiating from the centre of each flower guide insects to the nectar. We can't normally 'see' UV light, but insects can.*

49

pollen is left on that flower's sticky stigma. Seed formation can now begin.

Other plants simply rely on the wind to spread their pollen to other flowers. These include many of the trees and grasses, and their flowers are typically quite small, dull in colour, and have no scent or nectar. They simply do not need these 'extras'. To cut down the chances of their flowers pollinating themselves, many of these species have completely separate male and female plants. This happens in nettles, poplar trees and many palms. Others have separate male and female flowers on the same plant. Common examples are pine trees, oaks and maize.

Some plants, of course, need to be able to pollinate themselves. These include what scientists call the 'pioneer' plants – the ones whose seeds drift in on the wind and take root on bare ground. There may not be another plant of the same kind for a hundred kilometres, so self-pollination is the only way to survive. For most plants, however, pollination by another plant offers a much better deal. It mixes up some of the genes – the biological blueprint of the plant – with the result that one plant may grow a little taller than usual, or turn out to be better at surviving long dry spells, or produce bigger and better seeds than the rest. This cross-pollination – the mixing of genes from two different parents (animal or plant) is what makes evolution possible.

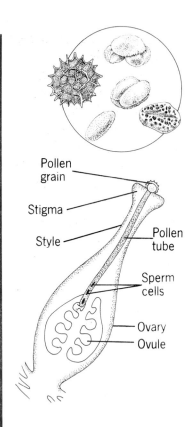

Pollen grain

Stigma

Style

Pollen tube

Sperm cells

Ovary

Ovule

The upper illustration shows the great variety in the shape of pollen grains. They are like miniature sculptures, and each will pollinate only its own kind of flower. The lower illustration shows how the pollen tube burrows through the fleshy style to carry the sperm cells from the pollen grain to the egg (ovule).

Blackberry

Flower

Fruit

Tomato

Flower

Left: *In many plants, the seeds are enclosed in fleshy fruits which develop either from the walls of the ovary or from the swollen upper end of the flower stem. Many fruits are good to eat. As the fruit develops, the sepals and petals wither and finally drop off.*

The illustration below shows seeds being dispersed by the wind, and by animals and birds. But the poppy relies on the 'pepper-pot' effect. When the ovary is ripe it swells into a dry hollow container with holes round the rim, and when it is shaken by the wind the tiny seeds inside are sprinkled on the ground.

Sowing the seeds

Once a flower has been pollinated by a visiting fly or bird or bee, it has completed its first task. What happens next is hidden from sight, inside the style. Each pollen grain starts to grow a long thin tube down through the length of the style, tunnelling its way towards the ovules in the ovary at the base. One tube gets there first, and the end bursts – releasing the sperm cells from the pollen grain. The egg is fertilized, and from that moment on the fertilized egg starts to grow into a seed.

There is just one job left to do to make sure that the next generation of plants will grow. The seeds must be spread as far and wide as possible, and once again nature has found a way of using just about every method imaginable. Some seeds have wings, vanes or parachutes and are carried on the wind. Others drift on the waters of rivers and lakes. Some are sticky, or covered in tiny hooks that catch in the fur of passing animals, while many others are enclosed in brightly coloured sweet berries which are a favourite food of birds. The berries are eaten – but the seeds have a tough outer coat that is not digested. The seeds pass out in the birds' droppings – perhaps hundreds of kilometres away.

Ash seeds

Thistle seeds

Poppy

Burdock

Bird

Mouse

Blackberries

Dandelion seeds

51

Shoot
(plumule)

Cotyledon

Root
(radicle)

Above: *Peel the skin from a pea or bean and you can see the shoot and root of the plant embryo nestling between the food-packed 'cotyledons'.*

Below: *When a french bean germinates, the case splits and the root starts to grow downwards. It quickly forms a firm anchor and starts to absorb water. The stem just above the root then starts to grow – arching upwards through the soil and pulling the cotyledons behind it. The tender first leaves of the plant, hidden between the cotyledons, are pulled to the surface without being damaged. Once clear of the soil, the leaves open, turn green, and start to photo-synthesize – make food for the plant.*

What's in a seed?

A seed is like a miniature life-support capsule. Inside its tough outer casing lies a tiny plant embryo – a baby plant, complete with the beginnings of its first root and shoot and a supply of food to give it a start in life.

Most seeds are fairly dry when they are first released from the parent plant and scattered on the ground, and in that state they will not grow. The first thing they must do is take in water through a tiny hole in the seed-case. This makes the cells of the seed swell up to their full size, and also starts up the seed's internal chemical processes so that it can 'unlock' its food store and use it to start growing. In some ways it is a race against time. The food supply in a seed is quite small, so the young plant has to get its shoot to the surface as fast as possible so that its leaves can start making their own supplies of sugar and starch.

But how does the tiny shoot know which way to grow when it is underneath the soil in total darkness? The answer is that the cells in the plant's roots and shoots contain very sensitive gravity detectors. Just as a blind-folded person knows when he or she is upside down, so the plant 'knows' which way is 'up' for the shoot and 'down' for the root. These detectors are very sensitive, and the plant will alter its direction quite quickly if it is placed in an unnatural position – for example by placing a pot-plant on

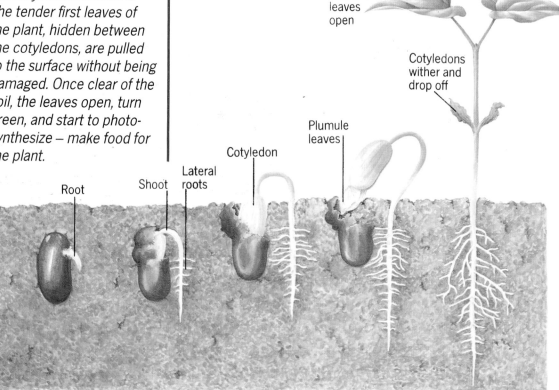

Plumule
leaves
open

Cotyledons
wither and
drop off

Plumule
leaves

Cotyledon

Root

Shoot

Lateral
roots

its side. You can see what happens on this page (right).

Plants are also very sensitive to light, and will turn their leaves towards the Sun in order to catch as much of the energy-giving sunlight as possible. Seedlings grown on a window-sill will lean towards the light, and if their tray is turned around, facing them away from the light, they will very soon start to lean back towards the window once more (see below right).

Biological clocks and calendars

Even more surprising is the fact that many plants know what time of year it is – almost to the day. Some species produce their flowers in exactly the same week every year, without fail, no matter what the weather has been like. Others start preparing for the winter well in advance by making their winter buds or by packing their underground stems and roots with stores of food. None of this would be possible unless the plant had some way of knowing the time of year – and it does this by measuring the length of the night, which changes steadily throughout the year.

A plant measures the time between sunset and sunrise with its 'biological clock'. We still don't know exactly how this works – but it must be similar to the biological clock that tells the swallows it is time to migrate to Africa, or the internal clock that makes transatlantic airline passengers feel tired and unwell because of 'jet lag'.

Below: *Plants react surprisingly quickly when they are placed in an unnatural position. A potted plant, for example, can turn its stem and root through 90 degrees in the space of 24 hours if placed on its side like this.*

Gravity-controlled change of direction is called 'geotropism'

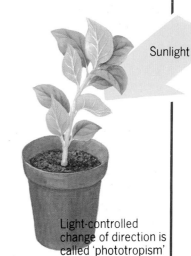

Sunlight

Light-controlled change of direction is called 'phototropism'

Above: *A fast-growing pot-plant on a well-lit window-sill will soon start to lean towards the light. If the pot is turned around so that the plant is 'facing' away from the window, the stem will immediately start to bend back towards the light.*

Left: *Sunflowers turn their heads during the day so that they always face the sun.*

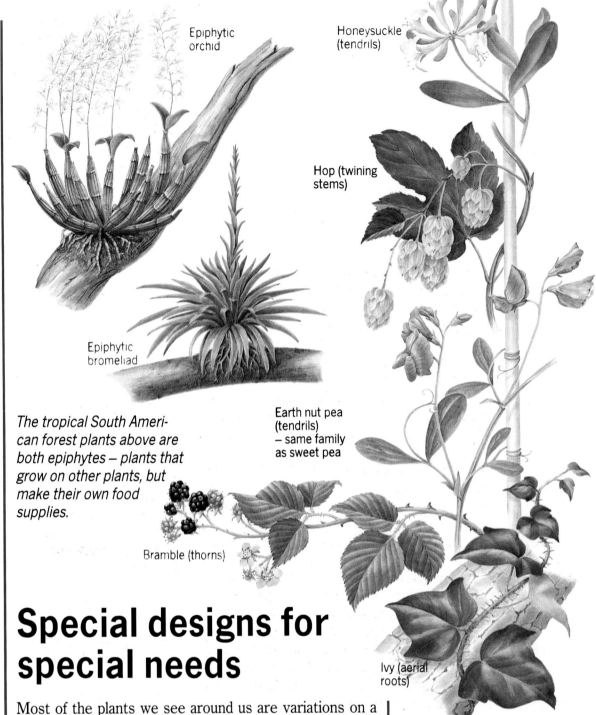

Epiphytic
orchid

Honeysuckle
(tendrils)

Hop (twining
stems)

Epiphytic
bromeliad

The tropical South American forest plants above are both epiphytes – plants that grow on other plants, but make their own food supplies.

Earth nut pea
(tendrils)
– same family
as sweet pea

Bramble (thorns)

Ivy (aerial
roots)

Special designs for special needs

Most of the plants we see around us are variations on a single basic design. They have stiff upright stems to hold up their leaves to the Sun. They have roots to keep them supplied with water and nutrients. They have green leaves with which to make food, and sweet-smelling flowers to attract the insects that will pollinate them.

But some plants have no stems. Others have no leaves. Some 'eat' flies and beetles, while others smell like rotting meat. These strange specializations are not just accidents of nature. They are special designs that have evolved to take care of special needs. They help the plants in their battle for survival, and in some cases enable them to live in extremely harsh and difficult conditions.

Above: *Common temperate climbing plants show a great variety of climbing methods. The hop twines around its support, honeysuckle uses coiling tendrils, ivy clings with thousands of tiny roots, while brambles hang on by sharp hooked thorns.*

54

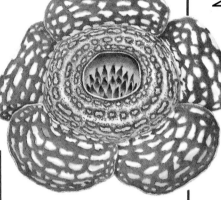

1 metre across

Above: Rafflesia *has one of the largest flowers known, yet most of the Rafflesia plant is never seen. It is a total parasite which grows on the roots of tropical vines in the jungles of Malaysia.*

Hitch-hikers and hijackers

Some plants make no attempt to build strong supporting stems. Instead of using up a lot of energy making woody material to hold them up, they use much smaller amounts of energy making special tools such as hooks, suckers and twisting tendrils, and then use these tools to climb up the stems of other, stronger, plants. The energy they save can then be used to grow farther and faster. Common examples are honeysuckle and ivy and sweet pea, and the rope-like lianas that hang from tropical forest trees. These plants have their roots in the ground, and they provide all their own food by photosynthesis.

Other hitch-hikers spend their entire lives far above the ground, using other plants for support but still making their own food. They take in water from the damp air through roots that dangle freely, never touching the ground. These plants are called 'epiphytes', and they are very common in the world's tropical forests.

Most of these plants are harmless, but some can prove quite deadly. The strangler vine, for example, starts life as an epiphyte growing on a branch of a tropical forest tree. The plant sends long roots right down to the ground, and when they reach the damp earth they take in a much richer supply of food. The vine grows faster and faster, smothering the tree with its dozens of interwoven stems – until eventually the tree dies and rots away.

Robbers and killers

The **parasites** of the plant world go even further. These plants do not simply grow on other plants; they feed on them as well, sometimes even causing the death of the unfortunate **host** plant. The common mistletoe is a partial parasite. It steals some food and moisture from the host tree by forcing root-like tubes through its bark, but it also makes food with its own green leaves. Other parasites, including many of our fungi, and the huge Rafflesia flower of the Malayan jungle, are total parasites. They take all their food from the host plant.

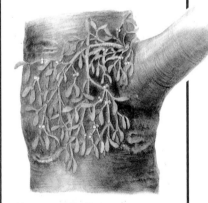

Above: *Mistletoe is a common parasite of oak, hawthorn and apple trees. It is spread by birds, who eat the sticky berries then wipe their bills clean against their perch – often leaving seeds behind.*

Hunters of the plant world

At first sight it seems very strange that some plants should be specialized to trap and digest living insect prey. But there is a good reason for this. Most of these plants are found in tropical forests and acid moorland bogs where the soils are very poor in nutrients, especially nitrogen. By catching flies and other small creatures, these plants gain a reliable alternative source of nitrogen – one of the main building blocks of all animal bodies.

The traps themselves are very varied. Some, like the members of the sundew family, have many tiny tentacles – each with a drop of sticky liquid at the end. When a fly lands it becomes trapped, and slowly the tentacles curl over and enclose it. The pitcher plants of southeast Asia have intricately modified leaves shaped like vases. A fly landing on the smooth waxy rim loses its grip and tumbles to its death in the liquid pool below. Most fascinating of all are the moving traps of the bladderwort and the Venus fly trap. The bladderwort is a common little water plant found in many parts of the world. It captures its prey in small bags which expand suddenly and suck the prey inside in a rush of water. The Venus fly trap is a spring-loaded device, set off when a fly blunders against the 'trigger' hairs inside. In fact, the Venus fly trap is a very smart plant

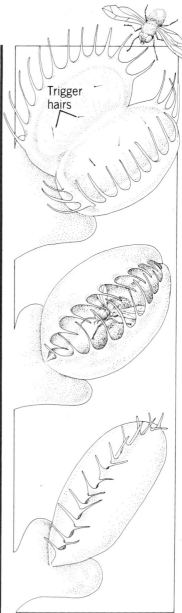

Trigger hairs

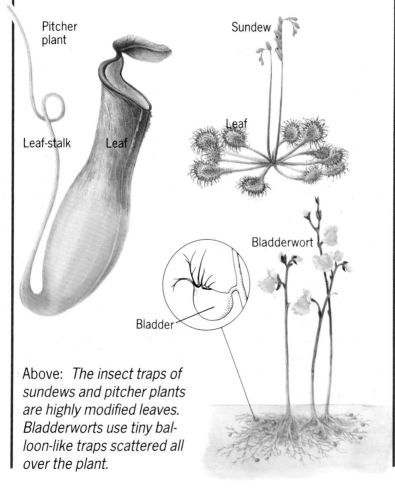

Pitcher plant

Leaf-stalk   Leaf

Sundew

Leaf

Bladderwort

Bladder

Above: *The insect traps of sundews and pitcher plants are highly modified leaves. Bladderworts use tiny balloon-like traps scattered all over the plant.*

Above: *The Venus fly trap is a spring-loaded trap. The two fleshy lobes are held apart by large cells in the hinge region which are pumped up to very high pressure. Inside each lobe are three long stiff trigger hairs, and if an insect hits these twice within about half a minute, electrical signals flash to the hinge cells, causing them to lose pressure and collapse. As a result, the springy trap snaps shut – and the insect is caught.*

Right: *The bee orchid is one of nature's finest 'con tricks'. The flower is the same size and colour as the female of a certain kind of bee. It even produces a scent very like the female bee's mating scent. It is all a trick. The male bee arrives and tries to mate, but all he does is pollinate the flower!*

indeed. It can count. And it has a memory. It can only count, 'nought, one, two', and its memory lasts for only about half a minute, but this is enough to make it a very efficient trap. When an insect hits a trigger hair, nothing happens at first. But if it hits a trigger a second time the trap snaps shut. This need for two touches stops the plant from wasting time by closing when a hair is hit, for example, by a raindrop or falling leaf. The half-minute memory is just long enough to guarantee that a fly stumbling around in the trap will be caught. It is almost certain to hit the trigger hairs a second time before the plant 'forgets' the first touch. However, if the insect flies off after one touch, the plant quickly forgets it and starts again when the next fly arrives.

Trickery and deception

Sweet perfumes and bright colours are not the only ways of attracting insects. To make sure they are pollinated, some plants go out of their way to attract insects with far less attractive preferences. Many insects – such as bluebottles, dung-beetles and fruit-flies – feed on animal droppings, rotten fruit and other decomposing remains. And sure enough, evolution has made sure that there are plants equipped to take advantage of this by imitating the smells and colours of these unattractive things. One of the most famous is a 2½-metre-tall Sumatran jungle plant called *Amorphophallus*, whose smell of rotting fish is so powerful that people have been known to pass out at the dreadful smell!

Other plants play clever visual tricks to make sure that they are pollinated. For example, certain orchids have flowers whose deep brown, purple and yellow colours and

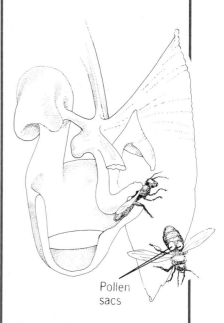

Pollen sacs

Above: *Small bees attracted to the bucket orchid by its scent, fall inside. The only way out is through a narrow tunnel, and as the bee squeezes through, the flower sticks a package of pollen firmly onto its back.*

Stinging nettle

Brittle tip

Poison reservoir

Above: *The tiny hairs on a nettle leaf are like hollow needles. If they pierce the skin and break off, poison enters the wound from a small reservoir at the base of the hair.*

thick velvety leaves look very like the females of certain kinds of bees and wasps. Each flower specializes in copying just one particular bee or wasp species – and it produces its look-alike flowers just at the time the male bees and wasps are looking for mates. The insects are fooled for just long enough. They land on the 'decoy' flowers and try to mate – and in doing so they actually pollinate the flower.

Designs for survival

Many plants have special modifications of their stems, leaves and roots to help them survive the very harsh conditions in desert, mountain and coastal regions. High mountain plants usually grow in dense low cushions to avoid wind damage. They have tough woody roots that spread out through the thin soil layer and into cracks in the rocks, and most have thick, small leaves with few stomata – pores – so that as little water as possible is lost.

Desert plants are among the most highly specialized. They, too, usually have fewer stomata than plants of the temperate regions. Many, in fact, have done away with leaves altogether, and consist of a thick swollen stem, rich in green photosynthetic cells so that it can make food, and filled with large water-storage cells. The outer skin is

Left: *Many plants are protected from plant-eaters by the powerful toxins they contain. Hemlock, deadly nightshade, yew and laurel are common poisonous plants in temperate regions. There are many, many more poisonous plants in the world's tropics.*

However, for many plants, such as the African acacia bush shown here, sharp spines provide enough protection. These plants are also important to many animals – especially in desert regions where there is little cover. For snakes, lizards, mice and other small animals, thorn bushes provide a vital refuge from the falcons, foxes and other hunters that threaten their existence every day.

waxy to reduce water loss, and in many species the skin is 'pleated' in concertina folds so that it can swell without splitting whenever the desert rains fall.

Sharp spines protect many desert plants from being eaten by grazing animals. But spines have other uses too. They are actually highly modified leaves. Some are tough and hard, but others are fine and soft and packed close together, or so fine that they form a woolly layer covering the stem. This 'wool' traps a layer of still air close to the stem's surface. As a result, less moisture passing from the stem is immediately blown away or lost into the surrounding air. It also provides protection from the searing daytime sun and the bitterly cold desert nights.

Desert plants have an astonishing ability to survive long periods of drought. Some of the small desert cacti of America, for example, can survive for years without rain. For most desert plants, however, timing is the key to survival of the species. The plants may remain dry and shrivelled, with no sign of life, for years. But as soon as it rains, the desert bursts into life. The desert plants pack an entire flowering season into a few hectic weeks, somehow managing to flower, pollinate, produce their seeds and disperse them during the short period when life-giving water is within reach of their thirsty roots.

Barrel cactus

Stone plant

Below: The seeds of desert plants may lie in the parched soil for years, but within days of a shower they germinate and burst into life, adding bright flowers to the enormous variety of desert plant life.

Above: Many desert plants have evolved ingenious ways of storing and conserving water. Barrel cacti store water in thick expandable stems, while stone plants use swollen fleshy leaves.

Other plants store water in specially modified roots. Some cacti stems store more than 100 litres of water!

4. The Animal Kingdom

More than a million different animal **species** are known to science, but they are very unevenly spread amongst the main animal groups. There are about 4200 species in man's own family, the mammals, compared with about 9000 different bird species and 20,000 different kinds of fish. These animal groups contain some of the most complex and highly specialized creatures on Earth, but in sheer numbers they cannot compete with the flies and beetles, butterflies and bugs of the most successful animal group of all. With more than 750,000 species studied so far, the insects easily outnumber all other animal and plant species added together!

The smallest animals are usually the simplest. Smallest of all are the microscopic dots of jelly-like material that float in the air and water. Food, water and life-giving oxygen pass easily into their bodies, and they have no need for complicated stomachs or lungs or blood circulation systems. For larger animals these systems are essential to keep muscles and internal organs supplied with fuel, and to carry away waste materials.

Larger animals also have a rigid framework – a **skeleton** – of bone and cartilage that supports some of their weight and provides anchor points for their muscles. This skeleton is usually *inside* the body and so it grows along with the body. However, three-quarters of the animal species wear their skeletons on the *outside* – like a suit of armour. In most respects it does exactly the same job as an internal skeleton. It also provides protection for the soft parts of the animal. But it cannot keep pace with the animal's growth – and that is why crabs, lobsters, scorpions and insects have to shed their skin at various times in their lives, keeping away from predators until the soft new skin hardens into the next suit of armour.

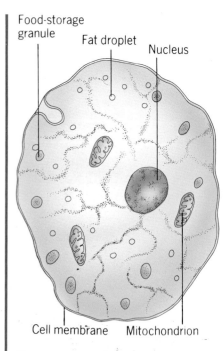

Food-storage granule · Fat droplet · Nucleus · Cell membrane · Mitochondrion

The typical animal cell shown above has no rigid outer wall. It can be almost any shape, and some – like the white cells in our blood – can change shape in order to squeeze between other cells. Like plant cells (p.28), animal cells are controlled by a large nucleus. They also contain food stores, and mitochondria where chemical processes take place.

Above: *The gemsbok is a large African antelope that is specially adapted for life in desert regions. Herds of 30–40 roam the red dunes of the Kalahari. The animals feed on the coarse desert grasses and on wild fruit such as melons and cucumbers. These provide most of their water needs, so the animals can survive long periods of drought.*

Right: *The Spanish Imperial Eagle is Europe's largest bird of prey. It is now rare in Spain, and officially protected, but is more common in eastern Europe.*

Animals under the microscope

The simplest forms of animal life consist of just a single living cell. They are called **protozoans**, meaning 'first animals', and more than 50,000 different species exist all over the world in the soil and water and as parasites on other animals.

Moving around

Some protozoans, like the pond amoeba, have a very elastic cell wall. To move about, part of the body is extended in a leg-like blob. The rest of the cell contents then flow into it, and the process starts again. It is rather like the movement you get if you handle a balloon part-filled with water. Other protozoans move by swimming along, propelling themselves through the water with lashing movements of their whip-like tails ('flagella') or waving motions of delicate fringes of fine hairs ('cilia').

Cliffs of microscopic shells

Some of these protozoa have hard skeletons. In 'radiolarians' the support is provided by delicate spines of pure silica. Under the microscope these structures are incredibly beautiful – like miniature sculptures in glass. Another important group called the 'foraminifera' ('forams') have tiny chambered shells of calcite. These silica and chalky remains form thick layers of fine mud called 'oozes' on the floors of the deep oceans. The forams that swam in the warm shallow seas of Earth's distant past now form huge thicknesses of chalk rock such as the famous white cliffs of Dover in southern Britain.

Above: *Under a powerful microscope, the silica skeletons of radiolarians are like glass sculptures.*

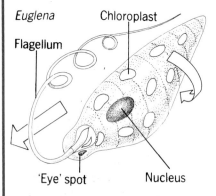

Above: *Euglena is an oddball. It swims with powerful beats of its whip-like flagellum yet it contains chloroplasts like a typical plant.*

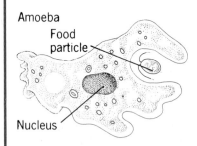

Above: *The pond amoeba eats as it moves – by flowing around the food particle and engulfing it.*

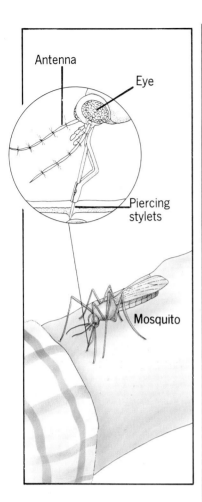

Above: *The deadly proto-zoan* Plasmodium *spends part of its life in the body of a mosquito. It is injected into the human bloodstream when a person is bitten by the insect. Once there, the* Plasmodium *cells multiply, attacking the blood cells and causing the raging fever of malaria.*

Right: *Few of the animals in the drifting zooplankton look anything like their adult forms. Most are colourless and transparent, and will go through several changes of body shape.*

Deadly parasites

Among the protozoans are a number of parasitic species that live in the bodies of other animals. Most of them are harmless, but they include some that cause very serious diseases in man. One, called *Plasmodium*, spends part of its life-cycle in the body of the mosquito and the other part in the human body. Once there, it attacks the cells of the blood and causes the disease malaria. Another deadly parasite is called *Trypanosoma*. It is spread by the bite of the tsetse (*tetsee*) fly and causes sleeping sickness in people and a fatal disease called nagana in cattle.

The ocean nursery

In addition to the true protozoans, the surface waters of lakes, ponds and oceans contain hundreds of other minute creatures, including the eggs and larvae of many much larger animals. This living soup is called zooplankton, and it is the first animal layer of the aquatic food chain. When seen under a microscope, many of these creatures look like monsters from a fantasy film. Others are very beautiful. Perhaps most surprising of all is that few of them look anything like the animals they will grow into! This is because, like insects on land, many aquatic animals go through various complete changes of body shape before they reach the adult form. Each one is called a **metamorphosis**. You can see some dramatic changes below.

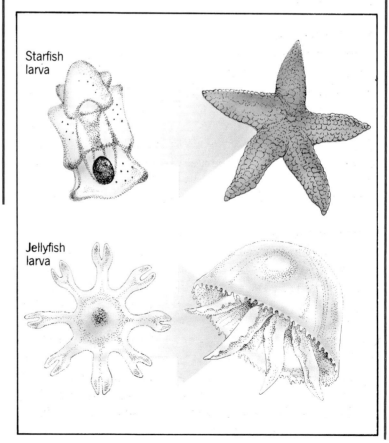

Starfish larva

Jellyfish larva

63

Animals without backbones

Of the million or more animal species that live on Earth, roughly 97 per cent are **invertebrates** – that is, animals that do not have backbones. This huge division of the animal kingdom contains a great variety of animal shapes and designs – from microscopic single-celled organisms like those we saw on pages 62–63, to complex animals like the octopus, butterfly and spider.

Most of the land invertebrates are quite small. They live in the soil, and beneath tree bark, and in other cool damp places where they can hide from predators. They include worms and millipedes, spiders and ants, and countless flies and beetles. Most are tiny, and even the giants amongst them are small compared with their relatives in the sea. The largest land snail, for example, is the 900-gram African giant snail. Its largest relative in the sea is the trumpet conch from Western Australia – a monster that can weigh as much as 18 kilograms!

Jellyfish, anemones and corals

Most land invertebrates have a basic body pattern similar to that of other animals – they have a left side and a matching right side, and a distinct front and back. But even this simple rule disappears in the sea. Here, many invertebrates are built on a circular or five-sided body plan.

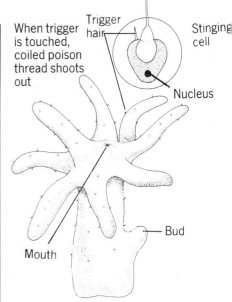

When trigger is touched, coiled poison thread shoots out

Trigger hair

Stinging cell

Nucleus

Bud

Mouth

Above: *Hydra is a fresh-water relative of anemones and corals. It lives in ponds, usually attached to water plants. The 7–10 tentacles are spread wide to catch water fleas and other small animals, which are para-lysed by the stinging cells and then pulled into the mouth. Hydra can repro-duce by a simple 'budding' process (where a small off-shoot develops and separ-ates from the 'parent' hydra) or by sexual reproduction.*

Below: *Hard corals, soft corals, sponges, anemones and a host of other inverte-brates make up the world of the coral reef.*

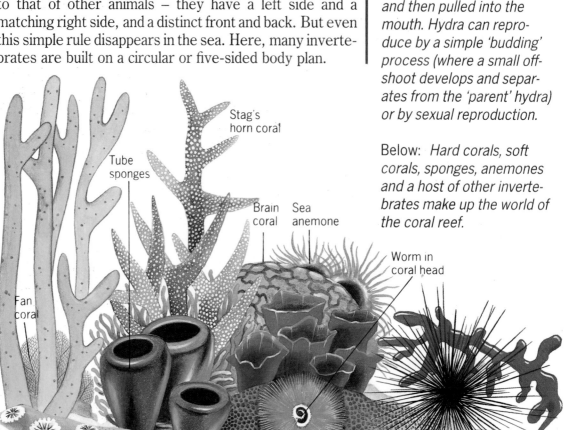

Stag's horn coral

Tube sponges

Brain coral

Sea anemone

Worm in coral head

Fan coral

Star coral

Lace bryozoan

Spiny sea urchin

Among the simplest marine animals are the jellyfish and their relatives. They consist of little more than a tube or bag of muscle with a mouth at one end surrounded by a ring of tentacles. These paralyse small fish and other prey with poisoned threads that are shot out like darts. The tentacles then pull the prey inside where it is slowly digested by special cells lining the wall of the body cavity.

The true jellyfish are free-swimming animals that move through the water with a pulsating motion of the umbrella-shaped body. They vary in size from a few millimetres across to giants of two metres. Another group, called the siphonophores, look like jellyfish but in fact are floating **colonies** of tiny animals called 'polyps'.

Most of the other animals in this family spend their whole lives in one place. Anemones live singly or in small groups attached to rocks, while the much smaller coral polyps live in enormous colonies. Each tiny coral polyp makes its own cup-shaped 'house' of calcium carbonate, and as these build up, layer upon layer, century after century, huge coral reefs are formed. The Great Barrier Reef, which runs for 2000 kilometres along the east coast of Australia, is entirely the work of these tiny creatures.

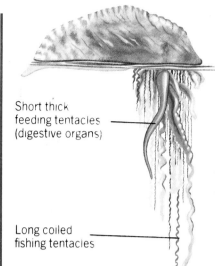

Short thick feeding tentacles (digestive organs)

Long coiled fishing tentacles

Above: *The Portuguese Man-of-War is not one animal but a colony of small, highly specialized polyps. This is the best known polyp colony. It is a native of warm tropical seas, but can sometimes drift as far north as British waters.*

Some of the polyps form the gas-filled 'sail' with which the colony is blown along by the wind. Others make up the digestive organs, the reproductive organs, and the long fishing tentacles which may trail 20 metres below the sail.

Left: *The anemone-fish can live among the stinging tentacles of a reef anemone because its skin is coated with a chemical that stops the stinging cells from discharging. The fish gains protection from its deadly 'partner', and its gaudy colours are a 'danger – keep away' warning to hunters.*

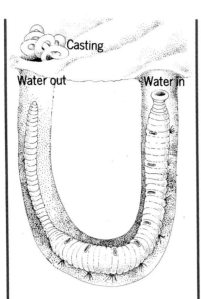

Above: *Many worms live in deep U-shaped burrows on sandy shores. The worm eats its way through the sand, and the sand passes through its body, leaving a 'casting' (coil) of sand at the burrow's entrance. The worm gets its food from water, drawn in through a funnel-shaped hole at the other end of the burrow.*

The 'lowly' worms

Worms may not be very exciting animals but they are a very successful and ancient family. There are four main groups. The first – flatworms, flukes and tapeworms – all have flattened bodies. Many live in ponds or streams, or in the sea, but the group includes many parasites such as liver flukes, and human tapeworms which can grow to many metres.

The true worms all have bodies built up of many ring-shaped segments. They include the common earthworm, which is so useful in keeping the soil churned up and ventilated. Most earthworms are less than ten centimetres long, but the giant South African species can exceed six metres. This large animal group also includes many marine worms, such as the free-swimming ragworms which use their powerful pincer jaws to catch their prey, and the delicate fan-worms which live in tube-like homes of cemented sand grains and extend their feathery tentacles to catch their food.

The last two groups, the roundworms and ribbon worms, are found worldwide. They are among the most numerous of all worms, and hundreds of thousands of roundworms inhabit one bucketful of North Sea mud.

Starfish and sea urchins

Scientists call this group the 'echinoderms', which means 'spiny skins'. They are all sea creatures, and apart from the sea lilies, which have stems attached to the sea-bed,

THE ECHINODERMS

Echinoderms have a 'radial' body plan – that is, instead of having a left and a right side they have sections, usually five, arranged around a central point like the spokes of a wheel.

Their remarkable body engineering includes tiny hydraulically-operated tube-feet, used for walking and feeding. These are operated via a central water-filled main. They poke out through holes in the sea urchin's shell and from the underside of the arms of the starfish.

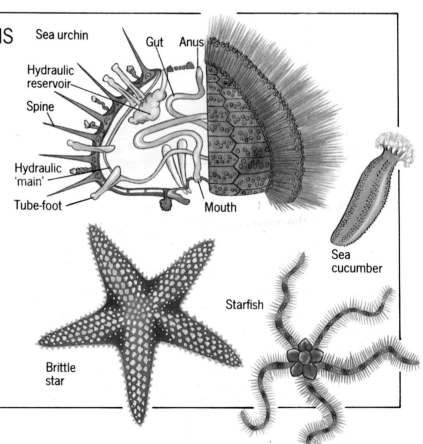

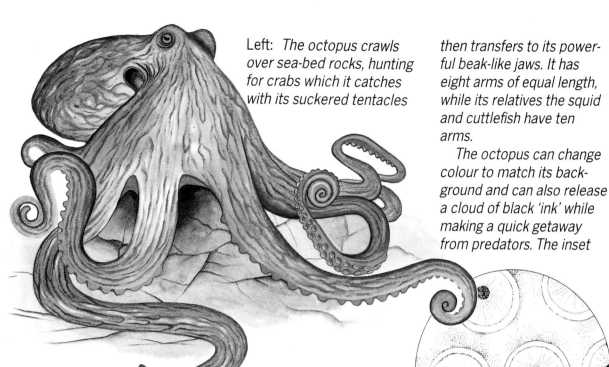

Left: *The octopus crawls over sea-bed rocks, hunting for crabs which it catches with its suckered tentacles* then transfers to its powerful beak-like jaws. It has eight arms of equal length, while its relatives the squid and cuttlefish have ten arms.

The octopus can change colour to match its background and can also release a cloud of black 'ink' while making a quick getaway from predators. The inset shows a close-up of the suckers underneath the octopus' tentacles.

they move slowly over the bottom in search of food. Sea cucumbers sift food particles from mud, urchins are scavengers of animal and plant food, and the starfish are hunters – attacking worms, shrimps and shellfish, which they pull open with their powerful arms.

Evolution has provided the echinoderms with some of the most ingenious body engineering in the animal world. Spines or spiny bumps give protection to many kinds of starfish and sea cucumber, but in the sea urchins the spines are long and very specialized. They are joined to the dome-shaped shell by swivel joints, and some species can walk on them like stilt-legs. In many species the spines are also tipped with powerful poisons.

Snails, clams and their relatives

The 120,000 members of the huge mollusc family are soft-bodied animals, usually with a large muscular foot like a slug, and a protective shell of some kind. This may be coiled like a snail shell or in two parts like a clam or oyster. But there are few other similarities between the different molluscs, for the variety of shapes in this family ranges from garden snails to giant clams and from gaudily-coloured sea slugs to streamlined octopus and squid.

Most of the molluscs feed by means of a rasp-like tongue called a 'radula'. It can be used to scrape algae off rocks, or even to drill through the shell of another mollusc. The two-shelled molluscs have no radula. They feed by filtering tiny particles of food from the water.

The snail-like molluscs move around slowly on the muscular foot. Some two-shelled molluscs swim along by 'clapping' their shells together, while others use the

Above: *Clams are two-shelled molluscs. They have small, primitive eyes around the edge of the fleshy 'mantle'.*

Above: *Sea slugs are relatives of snails, but most have no shell. Many are brilliantly coloured to warn predators that they are poisonous.*

67

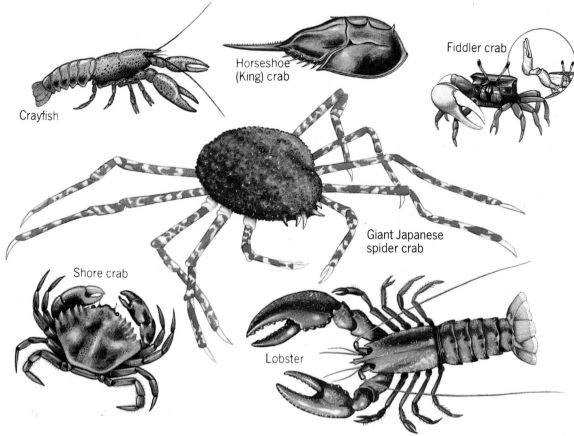

Crayfish

Horseshoe (King) crab

Fiddler crab

Giant Japanese spider crab

Shore crab

Lobster

muscular foot to pull them down into a sandy burrow when danger threatens. By far the fastest movers are the octopus, and its relatives the squid and cuttlefish. They propel themselves through the water at great speed by squirting water through a nozzle called a 'siphon'.

Arthropods – the world-beaters

If numbers alone were the key to success, the arthropods would rule the world. The name means 'jointed limbs', and this enormous group contains all the world's lobsters and crabs, all the spiders and their relatives, and all the insects: close to a million species in all!

Crustaceans – the lobsters, crabs and relatives

The odd-balls of the crustacean family are the barnacles. They alone spend their entire lives in one spot, filtering food from the water by means of feathery feeding arms. By contrast, most members of the family are free-swimming or walking animals with jointed body-armour, two sets of antennae, and also several sets of legs that are specialized for walking, swimming, carrying eggs, catching food or feeding.

Most of the crustaceans are salt-water animals but there are freshwater shrimps and crayfish, and even some land-living relatives – the wood-lice or slaters.

Arachnids – the spiders, mites and scorpions

The spiders, mites, ticks and scorpions form the second largest group of arthropods, ranging from mites less than a

The drawings on these two pages show some of the varied body shapes in the arthropod family. The group above are crustaceans, apart from the horseshoe (king) crab, which is a distant relative of spiders and scorpions.

The male fiddler crab waves his oversized claw to attract a mate and also to defend his territory.

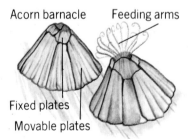

Acorn barnacle   Feeding arms

Fixed plates
Movable plates

Barnacles are the only crustaceans that do not move about. The soft body of the animal is protected by interlocking shelly plates which open only when the animal is feeding.

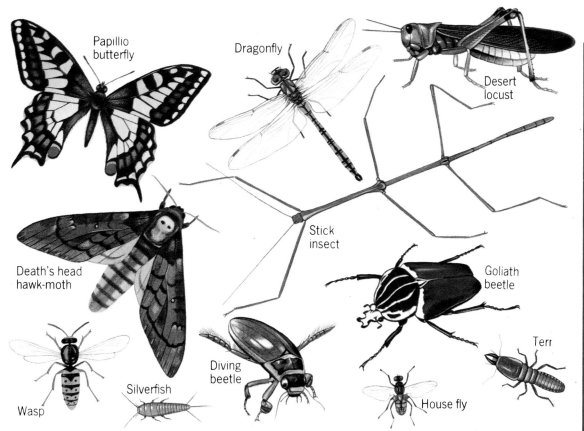

Papillio butterfly

Dragonfly

Desert locust

Stick insect

Death's head hawk-moth

Goliath beetle

Terr

Diving beetle

Silverfish

Wasp

House fly

millimetre long to the 18-centimetre African scorpion. Their body-plan has two parts. The front or 'head' section carries the eyes, jaws and four pairs of walking legs, while the rear part contains all the internal organs. None of the arachnids has wings.

Mites and ticks have mouth-parts designed for piercing and sucking. They feed on plant sap, blood and many other foods, and many are parasites. The spiders are hunters. Many use elaborate nets and traps, while others hunt by chasing or lying in ambush. Most paralyse their prey with a poison injected when they bite.

Insects – 750,000 and still counting!

The typical insect body has three sections – a head, bearing the eyes, jaws and antennae; a **thorax**, which bears the three pairs of legs and one or two pairs of wings, and an **abdomen**, which contains internal organs and may also bear special mating or egg-laying equipment.

Insects inhabit every part of the Earth. Tiny primitive springtails are found in the soils of the polar regions, while huge beetles, bugs, butterflies and other insects abound in the warm food-rich tropical forests. One reason for the insects' success is that they have evolved ways of using every kind of food imaginable. Some, like the mosquito and green-fly have hollow needle-like mouth-parts for sucking blood or sap. Others, like locusts, are specialized for cutting and chewing. Butterflies carry long, coiled-up drinking tubes, while many flies have a spongy pad with which they mop up their semi-liquid food.

Despite their great variation in size and shape, all these insects have the same basic three-sectioned, six-legged insect body plan.

Below: *Scorpions and spiders use powerful poisons to paralyse or kill their insect prey. Some species are dangerous to man, but their bites and stings are rarely fatal.*

Desert scorpion

Common garden spider

69

The first animals with backbones

Most of the great steps in evolution began in the sea, and the invention of the backbone is no exception. The first backboned animals, or **vertebrates**, probably looked just like most other marine worms of the time except that they had a main nerve cord running down the back. The links between these primitive 'chordates' and the first animals with bony backbones are still a mystery. But we do know that by about 350 million years ago, the four main groups of fishes had appeared. These were the jawless fish; the 'placoderms' – ancient heavily armoured fish, now extinct; the first 'cartilaginous' fish – ancestors of modern sharks and rays; and the bony fish, which quickly became the most widespread, varied and successful group of all.

Modern jawless fish

The only surviving descendants of the original jawless fish are the hagfish and the lamprey. Like their ancestors,

Mouth

River trout

'Teeth'

Lamprey

Lamprey

Above: *Once attached to its host, the lamprey can feed without interruption because chemicals in its saliva prevent the host fish's blood from clotting.*

Below: *Apart from the whale shark, these species are all hunters. The camouflaged carpet shark ambushes its prey on the sea-bed. The others follow the scent of blood or the vibrations set up by a sick or injured fish.*

A shark's teeth are arranged in overlapping rows. As the outer row wears out, it is replaced by the row behind. New rows grow throughout a shark's life.

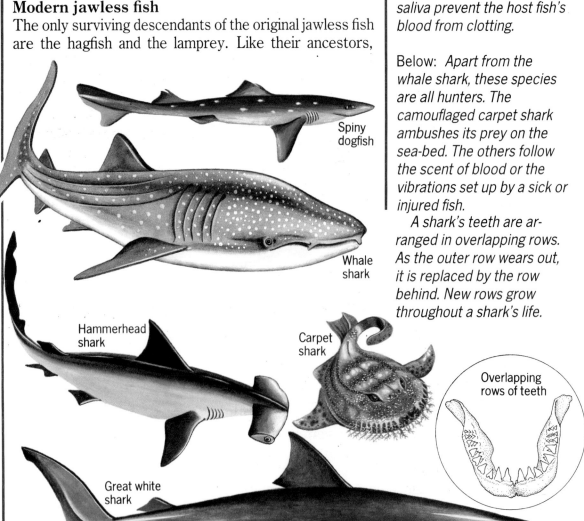

Spiny dogfish

Whale shark

Hammerhead shark

Carpet shark

Overlapping rows of teeth

Great white shark

these fish have mouth-parts specialized for rasping and sucking. They feed by attaching themselves to the body of another fish and then scraping at the flesh with the horny teeth on the tongue and the edges of the mouth.

The hagfish are found in all the world's oceans. They live in the sea-bed mud, and emerge only to scavenge for dead fish, worms or crabs, or to fasten themselves onto a living fish. The lampreys are mainly freshwater fishes. Many species are parasitic and attach themselves to fish such as river trout to feed on their blood.

Sharks, rays and skates

Despite their fierce reputation, most members of this family eat only fish and molluscs. The great white, mako and tiger sharks will eat humans, but the largest sharks – the 12-metre basking shark and the 15-metre whale shark – feed entirely on plankton.

The characteristic feature of the sharks and rays is that their skeletons are not made of bone but of rods of **cartilage**, or gristle. For this reason they are placed in a separate group – the 'cartilaginous' fish. Most of the sharks are predators, and their powerful jaws are lined with sharp teeth designed for stabbing and cutting.

Skates and rays are the other members of this ancient family. They feed mainly on small fish, molluscs and crustaceans, and some species can stun their prey with electric shocks generated by specialized muscles along the sides of the body. Another group, the sting rays, have sharp poison spines at the base of the tail.

Above: *The manta ray or 'devil fish' photographed here from below, may span more than six metres, but is a harmless plankton feeder.*

Below: *Sting rays defend themselves by lashing their whip-like tails, armed with vicious poisoned spines.*

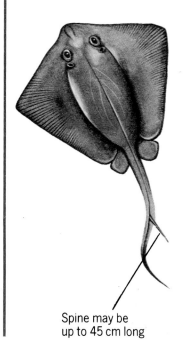

Spine may be up to 45 cm long

71

Bony fishes

The 'true' fishes – bony fishes – seem to have been successful right from the start. They very quickly found their way into every possible watery habitat.

The bony skeleton gives the fish's body great strength and flexibility, while an internal gas-filled bladder like a small sausage-shaped balloon automatically adjusts the fish's buoyancy, enabling it to 'float' at any depth. (The sharks have no swim bladder. They sink if they stop swimming.) Because visibility is poor under water, fishes rely mainly on pressure waves to find their way around. The line of pits along a fish's side reveals the line of tiny pressure sensors that are its main sense organs.

Another clue to the success of the bony fishes is their huge variety of feeding methods. Some sift food from sea-bed mud, others graze on water weeds, and fish like the pike are streamlined hunters. Some tough-mouthed species even eat living corals.

Below: *Shape and colour tell us about fishes' life-styles. Predators like the marlin are streamlined, while flat reef fish are ideal for passing through gaps in coral. The puffer fish gulps water when threatened and swells up like a balloon.*

Silvery undersides make the herring hard to see from below, against the sea's sunlit surface, while its dark back hides it from overhead seabirds. Bright colours such as those of reef fish are useless for fish of the ocean depths.

Mudskipper

Marlin

Herring

Hatchet fish

Catfish

Angler fish

Viper fish

Plaice

Living fossils and 'missing links'

The ancient group of fishes called the 'lobe-fins' was believed to have died out 70 million years ago. But the scientists were proved wrong in 1938 when one of these strange, heavily-built fish, a coelacanth, was pulled up in a fisherman's net off the coast of South Africa!

Other 'living fossils' are the strange, primitive, lung-fish of Australia, South Africa and South America. Because they have lungs and can breathe air, they can survive long periods of drought, sealed in mud burrows beneath the beds of dried-out lakes. They are the remnants of a group that was widespread in the Devonian period, and it may have been from creatures similar to these that the first land animals evolved.

Among the most curious of today's fishes are the mud-skippers of the Asian mangrove forests. These odd fish spend as much time out of the water as in it – breathing air through modified **gill** chambers. They often climb up mangrove roots, using their sucker-like fins to grip the stems. At other times they scurry over the tidal mud-flats, feeding on algae and a variety of small invertebrates.

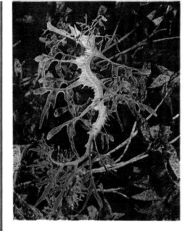

Above: *The leafy sea dragon of Australia is a master of the art of camouflage. Many loose flaps of coloured skin make it almost invisible among the beds of seaweed that it inhabits.*

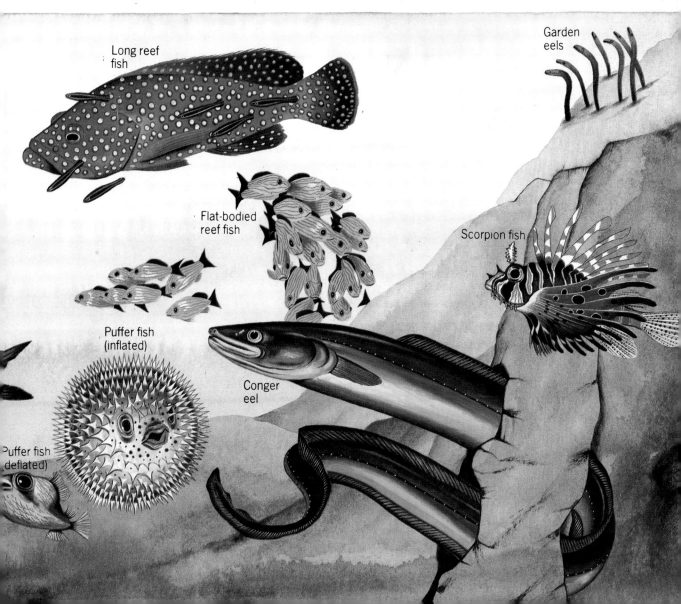

Garden eels

Long reef fish

Flat-bodied reef fish

Scorpion fish

Puffer fish (inflated)

Puffer fish (deflated)

Conger eel

Amphibians – between two worlds

Amphibians spend part of their lives in water and part on dry land. They are descended from a group of animals that flourished about 350 million years ago and included the ancestors of true land animals.

There are three groups of modern amphibians – the tail-less frogs and toads, the tailed salamanders and newts, and a curious group called caecilians, which have no legs. They look very like worms, and inhabit the damp soils of tropical forests in South America, Africa and Asia.

The importance of water

Amphibians reproduce by laying eggs, but as their eggs do not have shells they must be laid in water, or at least in damp surroundings, so that they do not dry out. Many species lay their eggs in ponds, or in damp soil, or in sticky foam attached to plants overhanging water. Other species, like the midwife toad of Europe, carry their eggs around with them until they hatch.

The eggs finally hatch into tadpoles, with fish-like gills and tails. They can live only in water, feeding on algae, but after a few weeks they go through a complete change of body shape and turn into four-legged, air-breathing adults. These are designed to live on land as hunters of slugs, worms and insects, though the larger species will tackle prey as big as mice and small fish!

Axolotl

Above: *The axolotl is a strange little salamander from the cold mountain lakes of Mexico. It is almost white, but retains the bright red gills of the larval stage even when fully grown.*

Below: *Most species of newt return to the water in spring in order to breed. The males of most species become brightly coloured and some perform elaborate displays to attract a mate. The male great crested newt develops a crest of skin along his back and tail.*

After mating, the female lays her eggs one at a time, attaching them to the leaves of water plants.

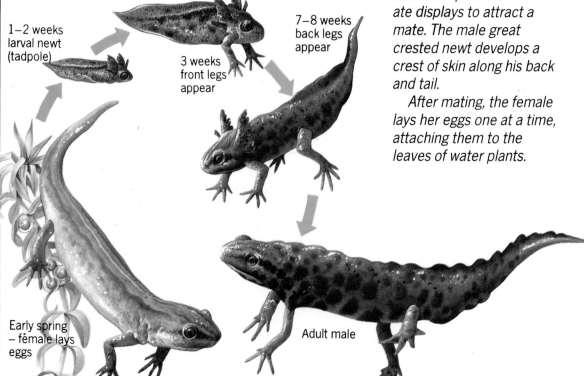

1–2 weeks larval newt (tadpole)

3 weeks front legs appear

7–8 weeks back legs appear

Early spring – female lays eggs

Adult male

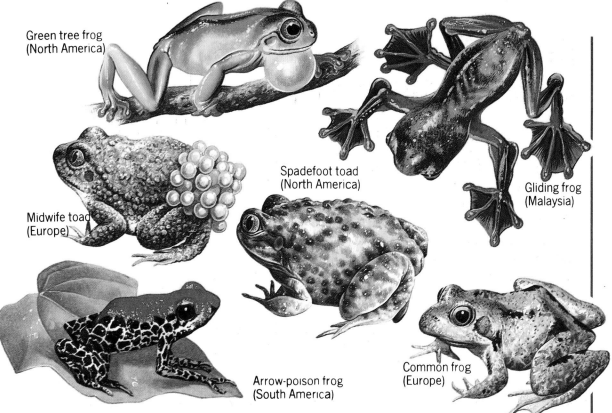

Green tree frog
(North America)

Spadefoot toad
(North America)

Gliding frog
(Malaysia)

Midwife toad
(Europe)

Arrow-poison frog
(South America)

Common frog
(Europe)

Although nearly all amphibians have lungs, and can breathe like other animals, they also breathe partly through their skin – but only if the skin remains moist. This is why frogs and other amphibians are so much more numerous and varied in the warm wet tropical regions. It also explains why newts and salamanders spend much of their time beneath stones and in other dark damp places, and why frogs are most common in long wet grass.

Frogs and toads must return to the water to mate and lay their eggs, and some species make quite long journeys – returning to the same breeding sites year after year.

Inviting sounds and warning colours

Many species of frogs and toads live in dense vegetation. Many are also active at night. Sound is therefore a very important method of communicating, and in some tropical countries the night air constantly rings with the piping calls of tree frogs. During the breeding season, marshlands in temperate lands echo with the deep-throated croaks of frogs and toads, but newts have no voice so the male newt makes up for his silence with brilliant breeding colours.

As well as being expert hunters themselves, amphibians make tempting prey for other animals such as snakes, birds, large fish, and mammals such as foxes and racoons. Some rely on a quick leap to carry them to safety. Others rely on their green or brown colour to hide them. But some have skins that produce foul-tasting, sometimes poisonous chemicals. Many poisonous species are brightly coloured as a warning to predators.

The illustration above shows some of the world's 2500 frogs and toads. The arrow-poison frogs of South America are among the most poisonous of all. Forest indians even use their poison on their hunting arrows.

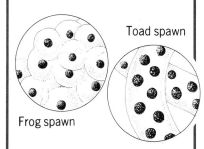

Toad spawn

Frog spawn

Above: *Frog spawn is laid in clumps, toad spawn in long strings. Otherwise they are the same. The male fertilizes the eggs as they are laid by the female, and several thousand may be laid at one time. However, only one or two survive to become adults. The rest are eaten by fish and birds.*

75

The reptiles – echoes of the past

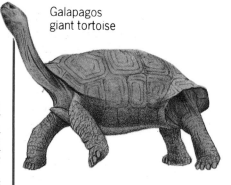

Galapagos
giant tortoise

The 6000 or so reptile species living on Earth today are all that remain of the vast numbers that dominated the Earth for 140 million years, from the start of the Triassic period to the end of the Cretaceous. They are a kind of 'half-way' group between the fish and amphibians whose lives are tied to watery habitats, and the advanced warm-blooded mammals and birds that can live almost anywhere.

Reptiles have dry scaly skin that is tough, waterproof and flexible and provides the animal with some protection. In the case of the tortoises and turtles it is modified into an armoured case enclosing the whole body.

Reptiles are often referred to as **cold-blooded**. Unlike **warm-blooded** mammals and birds, their body temperature matches their surroundings. This is why most reptiles either live in warm regions or hibernate through the colder months. However, they do manage to keep their bodies at a good operating temperature to some extent – by sunbathing in the morning to warm themselves up, and by seeking shelter later in the day if they over-heat.

One of the most important differences between the reptiles and the more primitive amphibians is that reptile eggs have leathery skins or shells, which means they can

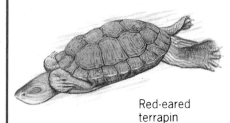

Red-eared
terrapin

Above: *Giant tortoises of the Galapagos Islands may have shells more than 1.5 metres long and weigh over 200 kilograms. The red-eared terrapin of North America is a typical fresh-water species, with a flat shell and webbed feet.*

THE OCEAN TRAVELLERS

Green turtles spend most of the year at sea, where they feed mainly on sea-weeds. Each year, in the breeding season, they travel hundreds of miles to favourite beaches on tropical islands. There they lay up to 200 eggs, in deep pits scooped in the sand. When the young hatch out they struggle to the surface and head for the sea, but thousands are eaten by birds and fish.

As if these natural dangers were not enough, green turtles and other marine turtles have been hunted by people for many years – for their eggs, their meat and their horny shells. Most species are now protected by conservation laws.

be laid on land – even in desert areas. Many reptiles do live in watery habitats, but their breeding is no longer dependent on water. They all lay their eggs on land.

Tortoises, turtles and terrapins

Tortoises and turtles have hardly changed in the last 200 million years. Their main feature is the domed horny upper shell, called the 'carapace', and the flat under-shell or 'plastron'. Inside this, the animal's body is arranged very differently from other animals. The ribs and parts of the spine are joined to the inside of the shell, and in order to breathe, the lungs are squeezed by abdominal muscles and movements of the legs instead of by movements of the rib cage, which is how most animals breathe.

Crocodiles and their relatives

One glance at a crocodile reveals its prehistoric links. It even looks like a dinosaur! It is perfectly adapted for its role as a predator in water. Its feet are partly webbed and its tail is flattened into an immensely powerful paddle. The eyes and nostrils are placed high on top of the head so that they remain above water even when the rest of the animal is submerged. Most obvious of all are the teeth. They are not designed to cut or chew but simply to seize and hold on. It tears pieces from its prey by twisting and wrenching. The female crocodile lays up to 60 leathery eggs in a hollow in a sand bank, while the alligator more often makes

Alligator
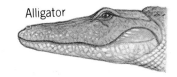

Crocodile
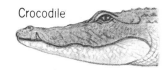

Gavial

Above: *The three main members of the crocodile family. Crocodiles have long snouts with one large tooth showing. Alligators have a broader snout with no teeth showing. The gavial (gharial) has an extremely long slender snout.*

Below: *Crocodiles by the shores of the Zapata Peninsula, Cuba.*

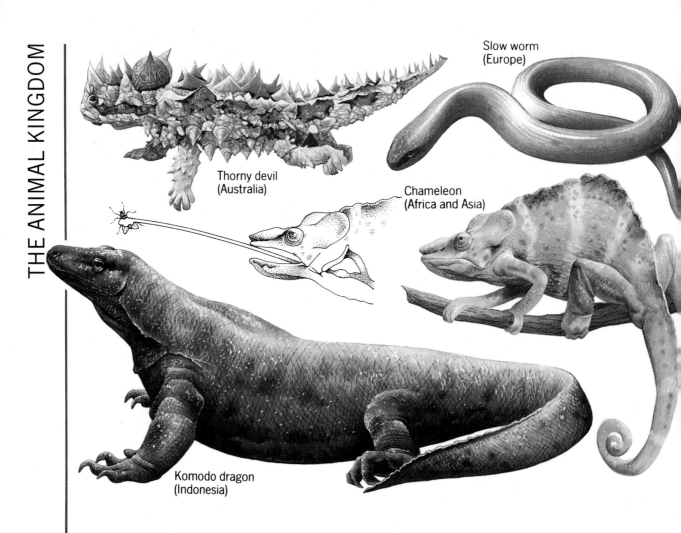

Slow worm
(Europe)

Thorny devil
(Australia)

Chameleon
(Africa and Asia)

Komodo dragon
(Indonesia)

a nest of vegetation. Both take good care of their eggs and young. The gavials (or gharials) are Indian and Asian species that are specialized hunters of fish, which they catch with a sideways sweep of the jaws.

The lizards and snakes

The lizards are a surprisingly varied group, ranging from tiny African tree lizards only a few centimetres long to the magnificent Komodo dragon which can grow to three metres and kill animals as big as pigs and young buffalo.

Many lizards are slender and quick-moving. Some have frills and flaps of skin that can be raised in threatening or defensive **displays**. The chameleons are highly specialized tree-dwelling lizards that catch insects with a long sticky tongue that can be shot from the mouth. Some Asian tree lizards can glide through the air on flaps of skin, and many species can discard their tails when under attack. The tail tends to twitch or curl, attracting the hunter's attention while the lizard makes its escape.

Most lizards lay **clutches** of leathery-skinned eggs, but several species (especially those in cooler parts of the world) keep the young inside their bodies until they are ready to be born. Some snakes do the same thing.

Above: *The world's lizards vary greatly. The chameleon catches insects with a sticky tongue that shoots out to almost half its body length. The thorny devil of Australia has grooved skin that channels rain or dew towards its mouth. The European slow worm is one of several species that have lost their limbs.*

Below: *The marine iguana.*

One of the most unusual of the world's lizards is the marine iguana of the Galapagos Islands. It is the only lizard that has taken to life in the sea – and although it actually lives on the rough volcanic rocks of the shore it feeds entirely in the sea, on submerged seaweeds.

The snakes are first cousins to the lizards and are the most recent of the reptile groups. Fossil lizards date back 200 million years, but the oldest snake fossils are barely half that age.

Most snakes have good eyesight but their most important sense is a combined smell-and-taste sense which many species use to track down their prey. Snakes (and lizards too) constantly flick out their forked tongues as they 'sample' the air and the ground for tell-tale scents.

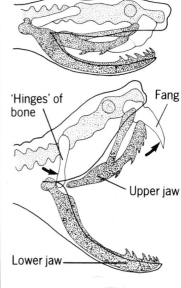

'Hinges' of bone

Fang

Upper jaw

Lower jaw

The pattern and colour of a snake's skin is often perfectly matched to its habitat. Many tree snakes are bright green. Desert snakes are yellow or brown. But the best camouflage of all is found in the snakes of the forest floor, like this reticulated python from southeast Asia.

Above: *The puff adder's poison fangs fold back when not in action, but during a strike they swing forwards to stab into the prey.*

All snakes are predators, and they are divided into two main groups. The constrictors, such as the boas and pythons, kill by squeezing and suffocating their prey. Like other large snakes they are able to 'unhinge' their jaws, and in this way can swallow very large prey. A big python, for example, can swallow animals up to the size of a small deer. The other main group is made up of those that kill by biting and injecting poison. In the most venomous species, the fangs are hinged so that they swing forwards and outwards as the snake strikes. Among the most specialized kinds of snake are the pit vipers. These have small heat-sensitive pits on the face, and can use this sense to track down warm-blooded animals such as mice, even in pitch darkness.

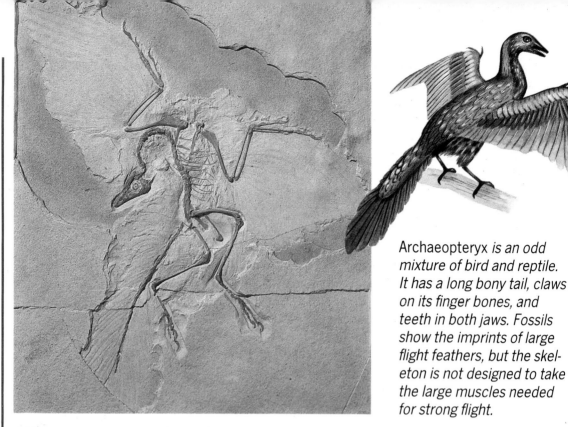

Archaeopteryx is an odd mixture of bird and reptile. It has a long bony tail, claws on its finger bones, and teeth in both jaws. Fossils show the imprints of large flight feathers, but the skeleton is not designed to take the large muscles needed for strong flight.

The arrival of the birds

The first birds appeared on Earth about 150 million years ago. They probably evolved from small dinosaurs that ran on their back legs like modern lizards do, and spent their time in the trees, scurrying about and jumping from branch to branch. Some may even have been able to glide on flaps of skin. At some point the reptile scales of these primitive creatures evolved into feathers – the one thing that makes birds different from all other animals.

A miracle of engineering

The first advantage of the new invention – feathers – was that they are marvellous insulators – that is, they keep the 'wearer' warm. The reptile ancestors of the birds were, of course, cold-blooded, which limited the range of habitats they could live in. But with a covering of feathers, birds were able to keep in more of their body heat, and so the evolution of feathers was probably a major step on the birds' road to becoming warm-blooded. And once they made that change they were able to spread into the high mountains, cold deserts and even the polar regions.

The other great advantage of feathers was that they made flight possible. One group of mammals, the bats, can also fly. They have wings made of thin elastic skin. But a bird's wing is a more complex piece of engineering, and can be tailor-made for many different kinds of flight.

Shaft

Barbule

Barb

There are several kinds of feathers. Long, stiff primary feathers provide the power for flight. Smaller shafted feathers like the one illustrated above give the body a smooth outline, and soft down feathers form a warm layer that is close to the body.

The whole of the bird's body is designed for flight. Its skeleton is very strong to take the stresses of take-off and the impact of landing, but it is also very light. The bones are honeycombed with air spaces to save weight. The neck and skull and legs are long and bony, with no excess flesh. All the bird's weight is concentrated where it needs it most – in the massive breast muscles that power the beating of the wings.

Flying uses up a tremendous amount of energy, so birds must eat a great deal of food, and digest it very quickly, in order to keep their muscles fuelled. Many migrant birds feed up on insects or sugar-rich berries for two or three weeks before their annual journeys. The tiny European sedge warbler, for example, almost doubles its weight in preparation for its 4000-kilometre flight to Africa.

A natural success

The first true bird was *Archaeopteryx*, a rather clumsy creature about the size of a magpie, which most probably flew from tree to tree by gliding rather than flapping its

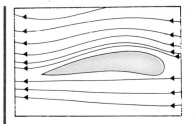

Air rushing over the curved upper surface travels farther and faster than air passing under the wing. This reduces air pressure above the wing, creating the upward force called 'lift'. It is this force that keeps a sparrow up in the air.

Vulture soaring on rising air currents

Tell-tale wing shapes. The vulture has broad splay-tipped wings for soaring on rising air currents while the swallow has the narrow back-swept wings of a high-speed aerobatic hunter. Each bird's wings are tailored to the particular kind of life it leads.

Hummingbird hovering to feed

Pigeon coming in to land

Albatross soaring close to wave tops

Swallow hunting high-flying insects

Above: *A colony of king penguins nesting amongst the tussock grass of a south Atlantic island. Most of the 18 penguin species nest on subantarctic islands.*

Ostrich

Cassowary

The ostrich and cassowary are fortunately still common, but many flightless birds are becoming very rare.

wings. There are very few fossil birds as old as this, but between 100 and 70 million years ago, many more species appeared on the scene. They included large flightless fish-eaters with toothed bills, and also the ancestors of gulls, pelicans and flamingos. Towards the end of this period many more new birds appeared – including penguins and divers, the first perching birds, and also several giant flightless land birds that very soon became extinct.

The greatest period of all for birds was about ten million years ago. All our modern birds were around at that time, but so were many more. Scientists estimate that there were almost 12,000 different bird species, compared with the 9000 living today. In the next few pages, and in Part 5 of this book, we will see just how well evolution has enabled birds to spread out and colonize every habitat on Earth, and every life-style.

Flightless birds

Although flight is one of the most characteristic features of birds there are quite a few flightless species – and they are found in a variety of habitats, from the southern oceans to grasslands, deserts and dense mountain forests. Most of the flightless birds are large, and rely on their size and speed, and in some cases kicking power, to protect them. The king of the land birds is the African ostrich. At 2½ metres tall and more than 120 kilograms in weight it is by far the largest bird in the world. Other curious flightless species are the **nocturnal** kiwi that lives in the dense damp forests of New Zealand, and the kakapo – a giant flightless parrot that inhabits the high mountain scrub forests of that country.

The most specialized flightless birds are the penguins. Their bodies are smooth and streamlined and their wings are modified into stiff muscular paddles, with which they swim and dive with amazing speed and agility. They are protected from the cold by a layer of **blubber** beneath the skin, and by their dense waterproof plumage. Emperor penguins can dive for up to 20 minutes.

Birds of prey

The vultures, eagles, hawks and falcons are a varied group of hunters and scavengers, found in almost every habitat on Earth. Largest of all are the condors and vultures which specialize in feeding on **carrion**. Next come the large eagles, including the magnificent harpy eagle of South America and the fishing specialists like the osprey. Then come the medium-sized buzzards, kites, harriers and sparrow-hawks, and finally the smallest members of the falcon family – the dashing and agile merlins and kestrels that prey on small birds and large flying insects. All these birds are recognizable as flesh-eaters by their powerful hooked bills and talons. Most also have large forward-looking eyes, giving them sharp vision for spotting their prey from high in the sky.

Swimmers, divers and waders

The waterbirds of the world are an enormous group, ranging from the familiar ducks, geese and swans of our rivers and lakes to the huge noisy **colonies** of gannets and guillemots that crowd so many of the cliffs of Europe and

Above: *The woodcock's bill is perfectly adapted for feeding in loose earth and fallen leaves. The tip is very sensitive to insect movements, and it can be opened slightly to grasp a worm or burrowing beetle.*

Below: *Many seabirds nest in huge noisy colonies on tiny cliff ledges.*

America. They include long-range 'loners' like the shearwater and albatross, and also those that love company – such as the flamingos that gather in thousands on Africa's lakes, turning the scene pink.

These birds, and the countless others that visit our estuaries, beaches and cliffs, have an enormous variety of bill-shapes, and this enables them to specialize on many different foods. Herons stab their fish prey while pelicans scoop it into the bill. Flamingos and spoonbills filter tiny food particles from the water, while ducks graze on water and riverside plants. Oystercatchers use a chisel-tipped bill to open shellfish, while godwits and curlews drive their long slender bills into soft mud in search of lugworms and other burrowing animals.

Woodland, farm and garden birds
The familiar birds of forest, moorland, grasslands and gardens are nearly all members of the passerine family –

Below: *Lesser flamingos gather on an African lake.* *This species is also found in India.*

Oystercatcher

Dunlin

Above: *The chisel-shaped bill of the oystercatcher (top) is the perfect tool for opening shellfish.*
Dunlin are often seen busily probing soft sand or mud in search of tiny crustaceans and worms.
Below: *Flamingos have complex upside-down bills designed to separate animal and plant food from the water and mud of the birds' lake habitat. Lesser flamingos feed on plant food filtered from the surface waters. Greater flamingos take fish, worms and other small animals from the mud of the lake-bed.*

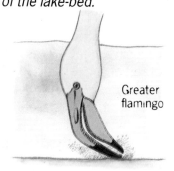
Greater flamingo

the perching birds. They account for 5000 of the world's 9000 species and they range from the tiny wren to large scavenger-predators like the raven. They are the most advanced of the birds, and in this group we find the most elaborate courtship displays, the most intricate nests, the most beautiful plumage patterns and the most musical kinds of bird-song.

Passerines are found in every country of the world, and include birds as different as the lyrebirds of Australia and the sunbirds of Africa as well as our familiar sparrows, blackbirds, wagtails and blue tits.

A world of specialists

Birds more than any other animal group make it easy to see the effects of evolution at a glance. The short thick bill of a European hawfinch immediately reveals that its owner feeds on tough-shelled seeds and nuts. The sharp hooked bill of an owl just has to belong to a hunter, while the slender curved bill of a sunbird is perfect for reaching the nectar inside deep-belled flowers.

But others are not so obvious at first glance. We must look for other clues. The crossbill, for example, has a bill like a parrot yet it lives in northern Europe. Only in winter is the secret revealed. While most other woodland birds fly off to warmer lands, with better food supplies, the crossbill continues feeding happily – using its powerful bill to slice into spruce and fir cones to get at the seeds inside. Its bill is perfectly designed to search out the only kind of seeds available in winter.

Below: *The woodpecker's skull and bill are specially adapted to withstand the repeated hammering as the bird drills into rotten wood to get at the insect grubs inside. Many species have sticky or brush-tipped tongues to help extract the grubs and other insects.*

Our family – the mammals

The mammals are the most highly developed animals of all, and the thing that sets them apart from other animals is that they feed their young on milk produced by the mother. Care of the young is very important in mammals. Most species produce only one or two young at a time – and in most cases they are quite unable to fend for themselves. Human babies, for example, are completely dependent on their mothers, while puppies do not even open their eyes until they are about ten days old. For this reason, many female mammals seek the safety of a den or burrow when it is time to give birth, and most will defend their helpless young fiercely if they are threatened. However, there are exceptions, and the most remarkable is provided by the large grazing animals of the grasslands, such as wildebeestes and giraffes. Within minutes of being born, young of these species can stand, walk and even run with the herd. It is a marvellous example of evolution fitting an animal to its environment. In open grassland there is nowhere to hide. If danger threatens from lions or hunting dogs, the only protection is to run.

There are many other differences between mammals and other animal groups. Mammals, for example, have a

Above: *For animals of the savanna there is always danger from lions, cheetahs and hunting dogs. To survive, their young must be able to stand, and run, within a few hours of birth.*
Below: *The young of higher mammals, such as primates, are quite helpless and must be protected for many months or even for several years.*

Chimpanzee

very efficient four-chambered heart. Their teeth are also very highly specialized, with cutting teeth at the front, holding or stabbing teeth at the sides, and grinding or shearing teeth at the back. Which combination of teeth a particular animal has depends on how it feeds. Cats have large canine teeth (fangs) for seizing and killing, and sharp cutting and shearing teeth for slicing through flesh and tough skin. Grazing animals have a simple chopping arrangement at the front of the mouth, and large flat or ridged teeth at the back for grinding their tough plant food.

Vision, hearing and the sense of smell are well developed in mammals, but the main difference between mammals and other animals is the brain. It is larger than in most other animals and much more complex – especially in the areas devoted to problem-solving and other 'thinking' processes. It is strange to think that such complex animals, including ourselves, have evolved from a group of tiny shrew-like animals that appeared alongside the dinosaurs 200 million years ago.

Mammals that lay eggs

The most primitive mammals are the monotremes – a small animal group found only in Australia and on the islands of New Guinea and Tasmania. These lands were cut off when the continents drifted apart millions of years ago. The fact that they lay eggs shows how closely related they are to the reptiles, but these curious animals are true mammals, for both the duck-billed platypus and the two kinds of echidna feed their young on milk.

Below: The echidnas of Australia and New Guinea are spiny burrowing animals between 50 and 75cm long, weighing up to 9kg. They are highly specialized to feed on ants and termites – rooting in the sandy soil with their fleshy snouts and scooping up the insects with the aid of a long sticky tongue.

Spiny anteater
(Echidna)

The extraordinary duck-billed platypus, shown below, is found in eastern Australia and in Tasmania. Its webbed feet, flattened paddle-like tail and broad bill are perfect adaptations to an aquatic life spent feeding on fish, freshwater crustaceans and frogs. The female lays her eggs in a nesting chamber dug into the river bank.

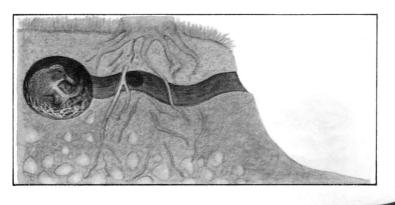

Duck-billed
platypus

Animals with pouches

The marsupials, or pouched mammals, are a kind of half-way stage between the primitive egg-laying monotremes and the more advanced 'placental' mammals which we will look at next. The marsupials give birth to live young, but instead of being kept inside the mother's body until it is fully developed, the baby marsupial leaves its mother's body very early, long before it is fully formed. At this stage it is blind and hairless and quite unable to survive on its own. As soon as it is born it crawls through the fur on the mother's belly and into the safety of the pouch. Once inside, it takes one of the 'teats' into its mouth, and there it remains – fed on a rich diet of mother's milk – until its development is complete.

Marsupials that live in desert regions or dry grasslands have evolved special ways of coping with their harsh environments. For example, as soon as a baby kangaroo has made its way into the pouch, the mother mates again. But her new baby does not begin to grow immediately. It develops a little way, but then it stops, and from then on it is held 'in reserve' until the one in the pouch has reached

The koala above may look cute but will defend itself very fiercely if threatened. It lives entirely on the leaves of certain eucalyptus trees, and unlike most tree-living marsupials, it has a pouch that opens towards the rear.

Right: *Red kangaroos inhabit the dry grassland of southern and eastern Australia. Big males may weigh up to 90kg and stand 1.8m tall. When alarmed, they can bound over the ground at 50km/h.*

These drawings show the main stages in the kangaroo's life cycle. In (1) the female is cleaning her pouch and the fur round the birth opening. In (2) the baby kangaroo is born, and struggles through the fur to the pouch unaided. There (3) it attaches itself to one of the teats, which will feed it as it grows.

After about 190 days the young kangaroo is fully developed. It can leave the pouch for short periods (4), returning to feed simply by popping its head inside the mother's pouch.

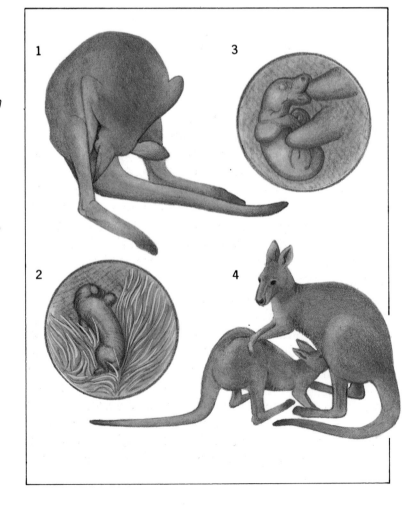

Left: *The wombat is a real powerhouse – a chunky, metre-long burrowing animal that weighs up to 36 kilograms. It lives in a maze of underground tunnels and feeds on grass, roots and tree bark. The wombat is a marsupial, and to suit her burrowing life-style, the female has a backward-opening pouch.*

Below: *Pouched mammals come in many shapes and sizes. The South American opossums are good climbers and often carry their young on their backs. The Australian bandicoot lives in dense undergrowth and so (like the burrowing wombat) has a pouch that opens towards the rear.*

full size, become independent, and stopped taking milk from the mother. As soon as this happens, the 'reserve' baby starts to grow again, and after about 35 days the tiny animal makes its way to the warmth and safety of the pouch. This method of reproduction is called 'delayed implantation' and it has great advantages. If there is a severe drought, many young kangaroos (called 'joeys') will die, but with this arrangement there are always 'reserve' babies ready to start growing immediately to replace any that have died.

The Australian success story

The marsupials have been around on Earth for more than 100 million years, and at one time they were probably the main mammal group. But two things happened to change all that. The first was the arrival of the placental mammals, which turned out to be much more efficient and adaptable and quickly took over in many parts of the world. The second was the break-up of the supercontinent. As Australia separated and drifted away, it took with it many ancient marsupials, and these were later able to evolve into new marsupial species, with very little competition. The various kinds of prehistoric marsupial included giant kangaroos, wombats the size of bears, and a marsupial 'sabre-toothed tiger'.

Today a few marsupial species survive in North and South America. They are mainly opossums and small shrew-like animals. But Australia is the marsupials' real home. Here they have spread out to fill every niche available. The kangaroos and wallabies fill the role of grassland grazers, the wombats are powerful burrowers, rather like badgers, there are marsupial versions of rats and cats, dogs and anteaters, and even a group of 'flying' marsupials – the phalangers – which can glide from tree to tree with the aid of flaps of skin stretched between their outstretched limbs.

Australian bandicoot

South American opossum

The 'higher' mammals

The expression 'higher' mammals has nothing to do with size, or where an animal lives – it simply means 'higher up the ladder of evolution'. In other words it describes the most advanced kinds of animals. Up near the top of the animal ladder are the 'placental mammals' – dogs and horses, whales and mice – and right at the very top are the **primates** – the very special group that includes the monkeys and apes and you and I.

The special feature of the higher mammals is something called a 'placenta'. It is a kind of two-way biological filter that joins an unborn baby to its mother's body. Through the placenta the baby receives oxygen and food from the mother's blood, and at the same time the placenta takes away the waste products of the baby's body. This safe and efficient system means that the baby can be kept inside the

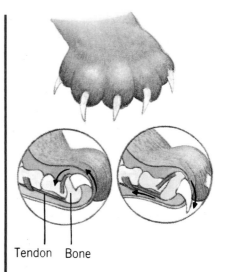

Tendon   Bone

Above: *All the cats are equipped with sharp retractable claws – claws that can be drawn back into the foot when not in use. This protects the claws and also enables the cat to move silently. In use, the claws are extended by tendons pulling on the toe bones.*

Left: *The leopard often pulls its prey into a tree, out of reach of scavengers.*

mother's body for many months, and this allows the placental mammals to give birth to their young at a much more advanced stage than the marsupials can.

Different shapes for different life-styles

Just as a bird's way of life is often revealed by its bill, an animal's way of life can often be guessed by looking at its teeth or feet or the shape of its head or body. The cheetah has the typical fangs and jaws of a meat-eater, but its long slender legs and deep chest also tell us that it hunts by speed. The beaver's chisel teeth give a clue to its feeding habits while its webbed feet tell us where it lives. The bush baby has the gripping hands and strong back legs of a tree climber – but one look at its enormous eyes reveals something else – the fact that this little animal does most of its hunting at night.

One of the most important animal specializations is hidden from view. It is the stomach! For animals that eat meat, or eggs, or insects, digesting food is not a problem. But for those that eat grass and leaves and tree bark it is another matter. These tough plant foods consist mainly of cellulose – and animal stomachs cannot digest cellulose, at least not without some extra help.

That help is provided by microscopic bacteria that live in the stomachs of cattle and sheep, goats, deer and antelopes. These animals are called **ruminants**. They are mainly animals found in open country, with little cover, so for protection they eat quite quickly and then find somewhere safe to rest and digest their food. The food is stored for a while in one part of the four-chambered stomach, where the bacteria go to work breaking down the cellulose. The food is then coughed up and chewed again before it is passed into the other sections of the stomach. So even the toughest leaves and twigs can be used as food.

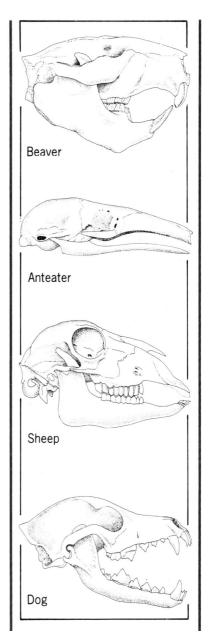

Beaver

Anteater

Sheep

Dog

Below: *The giant anteater lives in the grasslands and woodlands of South America. It uses its powerful forelegs and huge hooked claws to tear open the rock-hard termite nests, and then picks up the insects on its long sticky tongue. Although the anteater lives mainly on the ground, it can climb well and is a good swimmer.*

The skulls above belong to animals with very different life-styles. The beaver has sharp chisels for felling trees, and grinding teeth for feeding on bark. The anteater's skull is a toothless tube housing a long tongue. The sheep has no canines and incisors only on the lower jaw, but it has large molars with ridged surfaces, ideal for grinding down tough vegetation. The dog has the fangs and cutting teeth of a meat-eater.

Right whale
(baleen)

Sperm whale
(toothed)

Above: *Toothed whales such as sperm whales, killer whales and dolphins hunt a variety of prey including squid, young seals and fish. The baleen whales, such as blue whales and right whales, filter tiny animals (krill) from the water using comb-like sheets of whalebone that almost fill the mouth. Dolphins (below) are among the most intelligent and friendly of all animals.*

Back to the sea

Whales and dolphins are so perfectly adapted to life in the sea that it is rather surprising to discover that these ocean mammals are all descended from land-dwellers!

The modern whales fall into two groups. The whalebone – baleen – whales, feed on plankton drifting in the surface waters. The whale takes in a huge mouthful of water and plankton, then raises its tongue to force the water through sheets of whalebone that hang from the roof of its mouth. It is a very efficient filter system, and the stomach of a 30-metre blue whale may hold more than two tonnes of krill after a good feed.

The second group consists of the toothed whales, all of which are hunters. They are generally smaller than the baleen whales, and also much faster swimmers. The largest member of the family is the sperm whale, which can dive as deep as 1200 metres and stay down for up to an hour as it hunts for deep-water squid. The group also includes the killer whale, which hunts in packs, preying on smaller whales and seals. The smallest toothed whales are the dolphins and porpoises which feed on fish and squid.

The whales are intelligent animals, able to communicate over great distances by sound. Many make long journeys to and from their breeding grounds every year, and it was along these migration routes that thousands were killed each year when the whaling industry was at its peak.

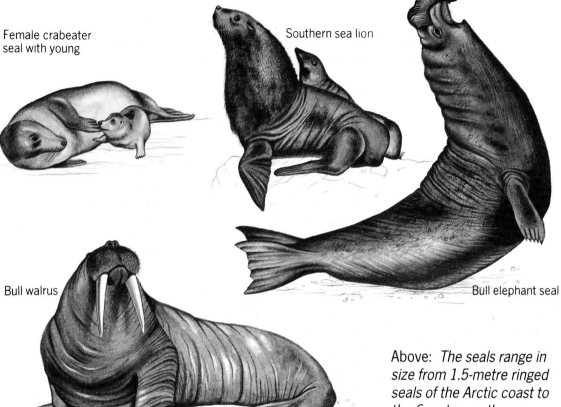

Female crabeater seal with young

Southern sea lion

Bull elephant seal

Bull walrus

Seals, sea lions and walruses

Like the whales, the seal family has suffered greatly from hunting in the past. Some species, such as the magnificent southern fur seal, were almost wiped out, but conservation laws now protect most of these animals.

Seals and sea lions can be distinguished quite easily. Seals are marvellous swimmers, but on land they wobble along clumsily on their bellies. Sea lions can turn their flippers under their bodies and can move quite quickly with a lolloping run. They also have small ears which are quite easy to see.

Altogether there are 32 species in the seal family. They are found in all parts of the world, but are most common in the cold Arctic and Antarctic waters. There, food supplies are good, and these remote regions still offer stretches of coastline where the animals can leave the water to breed without being attacked. And leave the water they must. Each year the entire seal population must come out onto land so that the pups can be born and cared for in their first few weeks of life, and so that the adults can complete their **courtship** and **mating**.

In most species the males arrive first, and the biggest ones claim **territories** on the beaches. The females arrive soon afterwards, pregnant from the previous year's mating. They give birth within a few days, and the pups grow very quickly on a diet of extremely rich fatty milk. Almost as soon as the pups are born the adults mate again, before heading back to their real home – the sea.

Above: *The seals range in size from 1.5-metre ringed seals of the Arctic coast to the 6-metre southern elephant seal, which can tip the scales at more than 4000 kilograms. The elephant seal gets its name from its huge fleshy nose, which it inflates when angry.*

93

Right: *The tropical 'flying foxes' are the largest of the bats. They feed entirely on the ripe fruits of forest trees, and may fly up to 80 kilometres in a night in search of food. The bats roost in large groups called colonies, and may festoon the branches of a tall tree like a collection of large untidy umbrellas.*

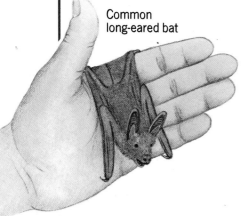

Common long-eared bat

Above: *Bats are so specialized for flight that their back legs are almost useless for anything other than hanging from a roosting place. When at rest, all bats hang upside down with their wings wrapped around them like a cloak.*

The larger bats are all tropical species. Those that live in Europe and North America are mainly small insect-eaters with bodies between 5 and 9 centimetres in length and wings spanning from 25 to 45 centimetres.

Mammals of the air

Of all the different animal groups, only three have taken to the air. They are the insects, the birds, and one group of mammals – the bats. Many other animals are able to glide from one tree to the next like living hang-gliders, using 'parachutes' of skin stretched between their legs or along the sides of the body. But this is not true flight. The best these animals can manage is a clumsy kind of steering as they drift down towards the ground.

Bats, however, are real masters of the air. Their wings are specialized versions of the five-fingered mammal hand, with thin, strong, flexible skin stretched over the long thin finger bones. Many species are extremely agile and acrobatic in flight – and indeed they have to be because many of them catch all their insect food on the wing. Their method of catching their prey is very interesting, and was only discovered by the use of high-speed film, which can be slowed down and studied frame by frame. Once the bat has chosen its target it swoops in to the attack, scooping up the insect in its wing or in the skin stretched between its back legs. Then, with a swift movement, it leans down and grabs the insect in its mouth. Most of the insect-eating bats are quite small, and they locate their prey using ultra-sound – a stream of high-pitched sound waves which bounce back off anything in their path, rather like a miniature radar system. A blindfolded bat can even dodge in and out of fine threads placed in its way.

SOUND NAVIGATION

The typical bat sends out short sharp sounds, made with the open mouth or the nose, that are too high-pitched for human ears. The sounds bounce back from objects in the animal's path, and are picked up by its very sensitive ears. The strange nose-shapes of horseshoe bats and the huge ears of long-eared bats are adaptations to improve the bats' use of sound.

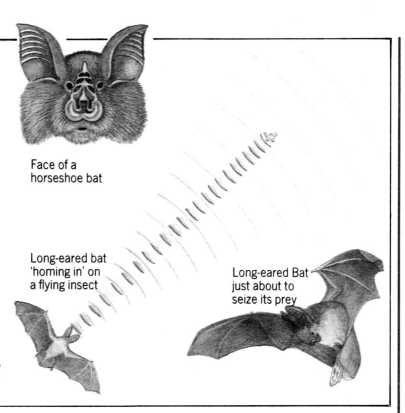

Face of a horseshoe bat

Long-eared bat 'homing in' on a flying insect

Long-eared Bat just about to seize its prey

Food for every need

Not all bats are insect-eaters, however. Between them they cover almost every possible feeding habit. Some feed on the nectar of flowers while certain larger bats are flesh-eaters, preying on frogs, lizards, mice and birds, and even on other bats. The vampire bat feeds entirely on blood. It lands on a sleeping animal or crawls up to it, and makes a small cut in the skin. The bat's saliva contains an anaesthetic so the cut does not hurt the animal or wake it up. It also contains chemicals that stop the blood from clotting. The main danger from vampire bats is that they spread diseases such as rabies.

The largest species is the tropical fruit bat, also called the flying fox because of its dog-like face and thick reddish fur. It has a wing-span of up to two metres and may travel many kilometres in a night in search of trees loaded with ripe fruit. Unlike the smaller bats, fruit bats do not use echo-location. Instead, they have very good sight.

A question of survival

Flying requires a great deal of food-energy, and so bats of temperate regions have a problem in winter, when there is very little insect food around. To avoid starvation these species hibernate – that is, they go into a deep sleep, hanging upside down in a cave or hollow tree or the roof of a barn, with their body systems set to a slow 'tick-over' rate. Several temperate species are endangered because so many old barns have been destroyed – leaving them with no **roosting** places.

Colugo (South Asia)

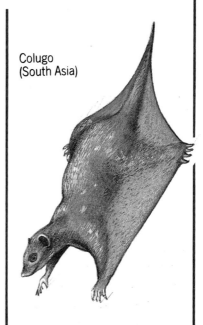

Above: *The colugo is one of the most expert gliding animals. It cannot fly, but by spreading the flaps of skin between its legs it can glide from one tree to the next. The colugo lives in the forests of southeast Asia and does not seem to be closely related to any other forest mammal.*

5. Animals in Action

Although many animals are 'loners', many others spend all their time in groups. Some, like bird flocks and antelope herds, are simply large collections of animals which offer a certain degree of 'safety in numbers'. Others, such as wolf packs and troops of monkeys, are much more organized, with recognizable leaders and complex rules of behaviour. Bees and termites are different again. Within their groups they have specialists to do various different jobs. Each way of life has its own advantages, and now that we have met all the main animal groups we can take a closer look at how they organize their lives, and how they behave.

The 'loners' of the animal world

Many of the simple animals that live in the sea and in freshwater habitats are true loners. There may be countless millions of them in a bucketful of water, but each one lives its life completely separate from the rest. They reproduce by budding or simply dividing, so they do not even have to get together to mate.

For most animals, things are rather different. Even if they spend most of their time alone they do come together for a short time in order to mate. For some, the meeting may be very brief indeed – like the airborne mating of many flying insects. Others may stay together for a few hours or days before the male and female part and go their separate ways. The male tiger, for example, never sees his sons and daughters. He would probably attack them if he did. In other species, male and female remain together until their young are ready to fend for themselves. Barn owls and woodpeckers, for example, are solitary birds as adults – but the pairs do not separate until their young have grown up and left the nest for good.

African weaver birds hang their nests of woven grass stems from the branches of savanna trees, but the social weaver bird goes one better: up to 300 pairs may join forces to build a huge communal nest (below) which may weigh more than a tonne! (The weaver birds are close relatives of the familiar house sparrow of Europe.)

Large elephant groups usually consist of females and their young, led by an elderly cow. The males live in a separate group, some distance away. Here, the group leader threatens an intruder while the rest make a defensive formation.

Safety in numbers

For many animals there is safety in the middle of a big flock or herd. The chances of being picked off by a hunter are much less than they would be if the animal stood alone. This kind of group living is very common in birds and fish and plant-eating animals such as sheep and antelopes. For these grazers of the open grasslands there is another great advantage in being just one of a large herd. With so many animals clustered together, there will be animals facing in all directions, and while some have their heads down, feeding, others will be looking around for danger.

Some animals feed in mixed groups, with one helping to protect the other. Baboons and antelopes often feed close beside each other, and the baboons' excellent eyesight and the antelopes' sharp sense of smell provide a very efficient warning system. In a similar way, cattle egrets (a type of heron found around cattle) are often found with grazing wildebeeste. They snatch up the insects stirred up by the animals' feet, but they also act as sentries – flying off noisily at any sign of danger.

For many animals, the only thing to do in the face of attack is to run. But some of the larger animals organize their groups into impressive defensive formations if they are threatened. Buffalo, musk ox and elephants form a ring, with the adults facing outwards and the young safely tucked out of sight on the inside. Dolphins, too, will work together in the face of a threat, and will even launch a joint attack on a shark if it looks as if it is going to attack a member of their group.

Musk oxen

Above: *When musk oxen form a defensive ring, all that an attacker sees is a wall of huge bodies and sharp horns.*
Below: *Prairie dogs live in huge burrow systems and often place sentries on guard at the entrances.*

Prairie dog

97

Drivers

Prey

Drivers

Main ambush

The lioness gets as close to her prey as possible by 'stalking'. The final attack is a powerful charge and a pounce. The diagram above shows how small groups of lions (red) may circle around a grazing herd (purple) and then drive the animals towards a large group of lions lying in ambush.

Everyday life in the wild

Many of the higher mammals live in family groups made up of one set of parents and their offspring, or sometimes of several sets of parents and their young. A pride of lions, for example, may contain up to 30 animals. The adult females hunt as a team and provide all the meat for the whole group.

Chimpanzees have a complex social life. The group may have up to 80 members and each animal knows its place. The leader is always a big male, and he keeps his position as leader by constantly showing off his strength and importance. Like people, chimps look after their babies for a long time after they are born. They protect them, feed them, play with them and teach them the rules of family life – and survival. A young chimp will stay with its mother for at least two years. It may then join a nursery band within the main group for a while before it is ready to join the main adult group.

Some animals make sure their species survive simply by producing enormous numbers of young. Many will die or be killed by hunters, but enough will survive to produce the next generation. This is the method used by most sea animals and insects. A half-way stage is to produce fewer young but to look after them longer to give them a better start. This is the method used by rabbits and mice, and many birds. The higher mammals produce very few young. Elephants, whales and chimpanzees produce just one baby at a time, and look after their young for several years. 'One at a time' is also usual in humans – but we care for our young for longer than any other animal.

Above: *Pelicans often fish in groups to increase their chances of success. The birds form a half-ring or horseshoe formation, which drives the fish into a tight group in the centre. The birds can then plunge their bills into the shoal and be almost guaranteed to catch a fish.*

TERMITE CITY

At the heart of the termite mound is the royal chamber containing the queen. Around it are nursery chambers for the eggs and larvae, fungus gardens which the termites cultivate for food, and dozens of storage chambers and ventilation passages.

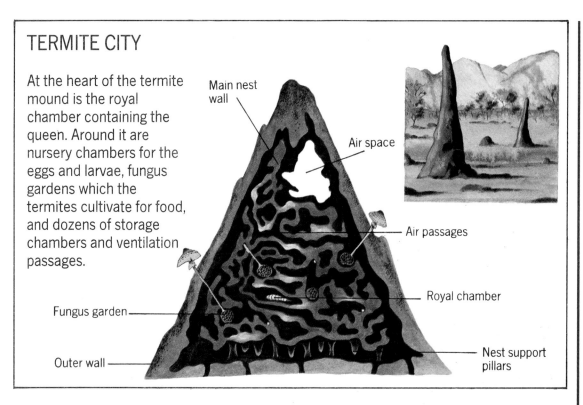

Main nest wall

Air space

Air passages

Royal chamber

Nest support pillars

Fungus garden

Outer wall

Animal teamwork

It is sometimes tempting to think that the law of nature is 'every man for himself' – but many animals work together in highly organized teams. In a large lion pride, for example, the hunting is done by the females, and they will often split into several groups in order to carry out a pincer movement, or drive their panic-stricken prey into a carefully-laid ambush (as you can see clearly on p. 98). Wolves and hunting dogs also work in teams, chasing their prey until it is exhausted, then surrounding it and attacking from all sides.

The hunting methods of lions and hunting dogs rely partly on **intelligence** and partly on actions that are **instinctive** – that is, actions that are done automatically, without thinking and without being taught. In other animal groups, behaviour is entirely instinctive – but it can still produce amazing results. Bees, ants and termites build complicated nests and underground cities, and their colonies contain specialists to look after particular jobs. In a termite mound the queen does nothing but lay eggs. Nursery workers look after the eggs and the larvae. Soldiers guard the entrances and protect the city from attacks by other insects, while teams of 'outdoor' workers gather food and carry it back to the nest. A single termite is not very impressive, but one or two *million* termites, working together, can construct a fully air-conditioned city with rock-hard earth walls standing more than 2.5 metres high, and with underground food stores, 'gardens' and water supplies.

Below: *The weaver ants of Asia work in teams to pull tree leaves together. They then 'glue' them in place using silk threads produced by their own larvae.*

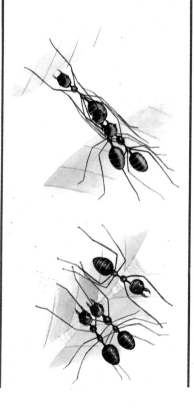

Animal language

Animals may not use words, but they do communicate with each other. Animals of the same species need to warn each other of danger, or signal that they are ready to mate, or avoid getting involved in unnecessary fights. Animals also use various signals to warn intruders away from their particular territory or their young, or to avoid being attacked by predators.

Animals communicate by sound, and by scent, and by a huge variety of visual signals. Some are simple facial expressions, such as the snarl of an angry dog, but others are much more complicated movements of the body, and may even involve special signalling colours or modified flaps of skin, or feathers. These various combinations of sound and smell and movement are called **displays**.

Private – keep out!

Many animals claim an area or 'territory' as their own, and defend it fiercely against any other animal that tries to move in or take over. Some animals have permanent territories. A pride of lions, for example, may have a 'home' area of several square kilometres. Other animals stake out a territory just for the breeding season. The aggressive male robin chasing all other robins from your garden is simply defending his chosen territory.

Dogs and tigers spray urine onto bushes and trees to mark their territories. Many kinds of deer have scent glands just below the eyes, which they rub against twigs for the same purpose. These special scent markers all signal to other animals that they have strayed onto some-one else's territory.

Curiosity

Happiness

Fear

Excitement

Charging display

Above: *Chimpanzees use various facial expressions to show their feelings, but it is important not to assume that they have the same kind of meanings as human expressions. Adult male chimps sometimes display by charging through the forest hooting loudly.*

Left: *The loud morning and evening chorus of the South American howler monkeys tells all other monkeys in the area that this patch of forest is private territory.*

Sound, too, is an important territory marker. The blood-chilling roar of a tiger, the evening and morning chorus of the South American howler monkeys and the bold song of the great tit all carry the same message – 'This territory is occupied – intruders beware'.

Fish cannot use sound, and scent markers would soon wash away, so those that do claim territories must patrol them constantly – often displaying warning colours or fanning out their fins to make themselves look big.

The never-ending game of bluff

The trick of making yourself look big and fierce is one of the most common tricks in the animal world – and it has a very sensible purpose. In animals of the same species it has evolved to avoid fights to the death between rival males. To show that he is the 'boss', the dominant wolf in a pack will threaten another male by snarling and raising the hairs on his neck to make himself look even bigger. Usually the other male will back down, using other signals to show that he accepts the leader. In this way the biggest and strongest dog will remain the leader. He will mate with the females and produce the next generation. Wasteful fights and serious injuries are largely avoided.

The same trick is used as a very effective means of frightening off attackers. An angry elephant spreads out its huge ears and the common toad gulps air until its body swells up like a balloon.

The European grass snake is one of many species that pretend to be dead if they are approached by an enemy. Many hunters will only take live prey, so this clever trick may save the snake's life.

Sudden changes of shape and size can frighten off an attacker or at least startle it and give the 'victim' a chance to escape. The one-metre-long Australian frilled lizard has a neck frill up to 30 centimetres across when fully opened. It also opens its mouth to display the bright yellow skin inside. The South American bush cricket can suddenly flash a pair of 'eye spots' if its 'dead leaf' camouflage fails to protect it.

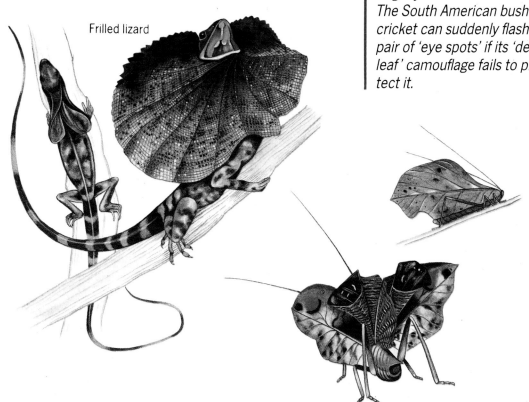

Frilled lizard

Above: *A pair of black-faced impala bucks lock horns as each one tries to make the other admit defeat. Battles like this are typical of herd animals in the breeding season. They make sure that only the strongest males breed.*

Above: *Firefly beetles can flash light for short periods. These on/off signals are used to send messages between males and females.*

Finding a mate

The noisiest, most colourful and most spectacular animal displays are those that take place at the start of the breeding season when the animals are looking for mates. In nature it is the male who does most of the showing off. His one intent is to prove that he is the biggest, the best, or the strongest, so that he will be absolutely certain to find a mate and so be able to pass on his good qualities to a new generation.

At this time of year bluff often gives way to real fighting, although one animal still usually backs down before serious injuries are caused. In herd animals such as deer, sheep, musk oxen and antelopes, the bulls fight by charging headlong at each other or by shoving and wrestling with antlers locked together. The winner gathers a large number of females into a 'harem' – and guards them jealously against all other males.

While the mammals are bellowing and fighting, male birds are dressed in their finest colours and are singing and strutting and performing all kinds of dances and flying displays. Some make presents of food to the female of their choice, while others make gifts of nest-building materials. Some birds, like the common woodland birds of Europe and North America, rely mainly on songs and movements to attract a mate, but others have much more dramatic decorations to show off. The frigate-bird of the tropical oceans has a pouch of brilliant scarlet skin on his throat which he can inflate like a balloon, while peacocks, lyrebirds, pheasants and birds of paradise are adorned with plumes and fans and ribbon-like feathers of every colour imaginable.

Day-to-day language

Once the noise and fuss of the mating season is over the animals settle down to raise their young, and new sets of signs and signals are needed.

Adult birds greet each other with special displays when one returns to the nest after going off to feed. When the young birds want food they, too, make special calls, or tap their parents' bills. As the young birds grow, the adults use different calls to bring them to food or to tell them to hide when danger threatens. Mammals, too, use a variety of sounds. Most use just a few squeaks, grunts, barks and whistling sounds, but the whales and dolphins have a complex language of sounds with which they are able to communicate over great distances.

For some animals the silent chemical languages of scent and taste are the most important. Some fish, for example, have a chemical in their skin that is released into the water if they are attacked and injured. Other fish react to the danger signal and scatter immediately.

Ants from the same nest recognize each other by scent, and if an ant mistakenly tries to enter the wrong nest it is immediately set upon by the guards. Ants will also leave scent trails back to the nest whenever they find a good place to gather food. This then makes it easy for other ants to make straight for the same place without having to waste time searching for it. Insects are incredibly sensitive to taste and smell. A male moth can scent a female more than a kilometre away, while butterflies can judge the sweetness of nectar using 'taste' sensors in their feet!

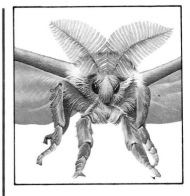

Above: *Many insects are camouflaged for protection and others are active only at night, so scent is an important means of finding a mate. The huge feathery antennae of the male North American moon moth can pick up the mating scent of a female moth at a distance of several kilometres.*

Right: *Many male birds rely on elaborate visual displays to attract a mate, and there is no finer display than that of the peacock as he struts about in front of a peahen with his shimmering tail fan fully raised.*

The courtship arena of the satin bowerbird is an avenue of twigs and grass stems decorated with stones, feathers and berries. Males work on the bower for the whole breeding season, during which they mate with many females. After mating, females build nests elsewhere for their eggs.

Architects, artists and builders

The termite 'city' illustrated on page 99 is just one example of animal architecture. But animals build many different kinds of structures. They build houses to live in and shelters for their eggs and young. They build an amazing variety of traps and snares with which to catch their food, and some even build special areas called 'arenas' in which to perform their courtship displays.

Artists and stage designers

The courtship behaviour of the bowerbirds of Australia and New Guinea is quite unlike that of any other group of birds. Several other birds, including ruffs and grouse and lyrebirds, use open patches of ground as arenas – but the bowerbirds go one better and actually build elaborately decorated stages for their performances. The bowers are made out of grass and twigs and are decorated with flowers and shells and coloured berries, and sometimes even with man-made objects such as shotgun cartridge cases and coloured bottle tops. The simplest bowers consist of two walls of interwoven twigs. The most complex are like circular grass huts built around the base of a small tree. Because of their shape they are often referred to as 'maypole bowers'.

Male weaver birds of the African grassland build up their woven 'baskets' from a hanging loop of twisted grass stems (see also page 96).

The South American oven-bird builds a mud nest on top of a fence post or on a branch. A curved passage links the entrance with the main, grass-lined chamber.

The penduline tit is one of Europe's most skilful nest builders. The intricately woven nest, made of grass, is often built hanging over water in a reed-bed.

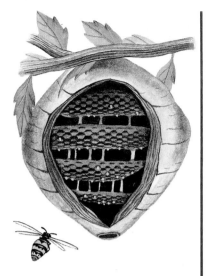

The nests of social wasps like the hornet contain several carefully constructed horizontal combs with the cells facing downwards. The larvae are fed on chewed-up insects, brought to the nest by the workers. The nest has just one entrance hole – in the centre at the bottom – and the whole structure is made out of 'paper'.

The art of the nest-maker

Birds make nests from every material imaginable. The simple cup-shaped nests of our garden and woodland birds are beautifully constructed from twigs and grass stems, snugly lined with moss, wool and feathers. But many nests are far more elaborate. For example, Indian tailor-birds stitch the edges of living leaves together with spider silk or plant fibres. Perhaps most curious of all are the white, almost-transparent cups of hardened **saliva** stuck high on the walls of forest caves by the cave-dwelling swifts of Asia. One of these is shown below, along with some other ingenious builders.

Potters and paper-makers

Mud is a very useful building material. The female potter wasp collects little balls of sticky mud and fashions them into strips which she builds up, layer upon layer, to make a small bottle-shaped clay pot. Before finishing the pot she flies off and catches several beetle larvae and caterpillars, paralysing each one with her sting but not killing it. These are placed in the pot, then an egg is laid and the pot is sealed up. The wasp's job is completed and so she flies off, leaving the wasp larva to hatch out, right next to its store of fresh food!

Some of the most delicate animal homes are the paper nests of the hornet and its relatives. Each nest starts as a simple hollow ball containing a structure called a 'comb'. For the first batch of eggs the comb starts out as a small

The horned coot inhabits the shallow lakes of the high Andes. It lays its eggs on an artificial island of stones. This can measure up to 4 metres across.

Just before the female hornbill, of Africa and Asia, lays her eggs, the male seals her inside the nest hole by plastering up the entrance hole with mud.

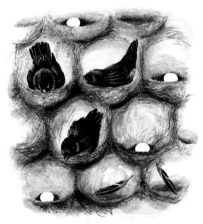

To build its highly unusual nest, the cave swift swoops back and forth, adding a strand of saliva each time it reaches the chosen spot on the cave wall.

structure made up of just a few wax units called cells. But as each generation hatches, the hornets set to work extending the nest and the comb – until it becomes a multi-storey tenement housing many thousands of workers – building, repairing and caring for the larvae. The whole nest structure is made of paper – tiny particles of wood that have been scraped from a log or fence post and mixed with saliva.

Sticks and stones and bubble nests

The watery world also has its share of architects and builders. The male stickleback makes a tunnel-shaped nest of algae and bits of water-weed, glued together with a sticky liquid produced in his body. The nest starts as a solid oval lump the size of a walnut, but once the first stage is completed the stickleback bores a hole through the middle to turn it into a tunnel. The female swims into the nest and lays her eggs, and immediately afterwards the male follows and fertilizes them.

Many water animals use small pebbles and pieces of shell for protection. The larva of the caddis fly, for example, hatches out of its egg on the bed of a stream and immediately weaves a silken tube around its body. This is then covered with small stones, bits of shell and plant debris until the soft-bodied larva is armoured and camouflaged as well.

The paradise fish of tropical Asia have a very different method. The male blows a raft of bubbles which floats on the lake surface. When the female lays her oily eggs they float upwards into the protective foam, and there the male guards them until they hatch.

Above: *Once the female stickleback has laid her eggs in the tunnel-nest, she leaves. The male then takes over and guards the eggs until the young hatch out.*

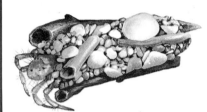

Above: *The larva of the caddis fly has a soft body with no natural protection, so it spins a cocoon of silk and covers it with small stones and bits of shell and plant stems. Each of the many different species has its own architectural 'style'.*

Left: *The beaver dam and lodge is a masterpiece of animal engineering. The largest dams are hundreds of metres long and more than a metre high. Dams of that size are the work of large colonies of beavers, working together over a period of many years.*

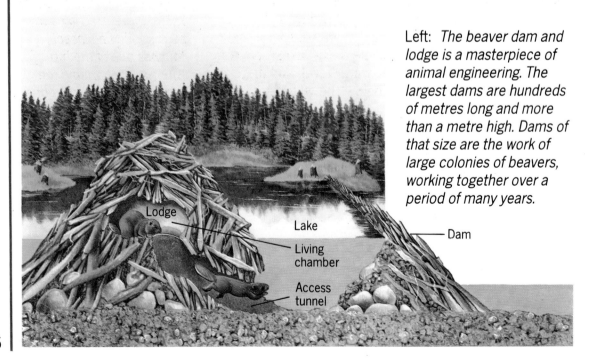

Lodge

Lake

Living chamber

Access tunnel

Dam

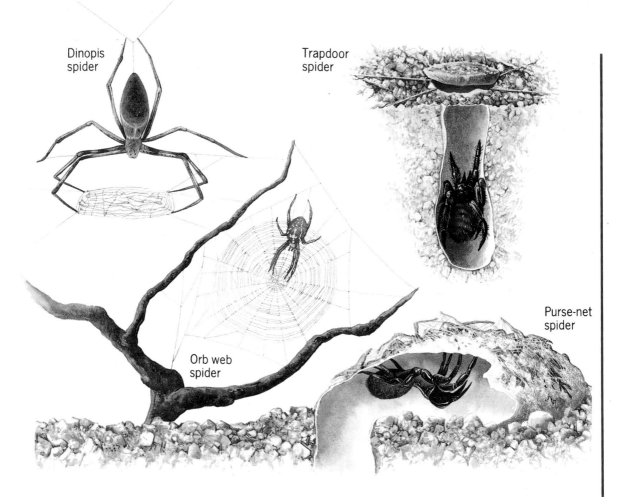

Dinopis spider

Trapdoor spider

Orb web spider

Purse-net spider

The master builders of the water world must, however, be the beavers. These powerful chisel-toothed **rodents** build dams of felled trees across their home rivers in order to control the water level and create a permanent lake. Building these huge structures requires teamwork, and several families will often share the work. Timber is felled, cut into suitable lengths, and dragged to the water. It is then floated into position and wedged firmly in place. The beavers actually live in a 'lodge' – an artificial island of interlocked branches in the middle of the lake. The living chambers are inside, above the water level, and there are many access tunnels opening below the water-line.

The deadly trappers

Everyone, at some time, must have watched in fascination as a spider has made or repaired a web. The fine silk thread is spun from glands on the spider's abdomen, and the spider can even choose different kinds of thread for different tasks. She has strong dry thread for the main supports, dry thread coated with drops of glue for the spiral trap threads, special fine threads for wrapping up prey and yet another kind for making egg cocoons.

But not all spiders make spiral trap webs. Some use sticky lassoos or throwing nets. Others lurk in tunnels and pounce when their prey hits a hidden trip wire. Spider silk is actually one of nature's toughest materials.

Because it is so strong and elastic, spider silk can be used in many ways. The Australian Dinopis spider hangs by a thread and throws its net over an insect passing below. The trapdoor spider hides in its lair and springs out if an insect touches one of the trip-wires laid out around the burrow like the spokes of a wheel. The European purse-net spider lives in its silken purse. If an insect steps on the purse it is 'stabbed' through the silk wall and dragged inside.

Armour, spines and secret weapons

Skin, scales, hairs and feathers can be modified in many strange and unusual ways, and for many animals the outer covering of the body provides most of their protection against their natural enemies.

Some animals are completely enclosed in a hard outer case. Clams and oysters can clamp their two shells tightly together, while various members of the snail family can pull themselves right inside their coiled shells and seal off the opening with a small shelly plate that fits like a water-tight door. Once inside, these animals are safe – except, of course, from those enemies strong enough to smash or drill right through the shell.

Body armour comes in many different designs. The 'tanks' of the animal world are the tortoises and turtles, crabs and lobsters, while the almost-square box-fish is the nearest thing to an armoured submarine in the animal world. Other animals have more complicated flexible armour. Like medieval knights they lumber along, not very agile but very well protected against their enemies. The large overlapping scales of the pangolin are actually very highly modified hairs. In other animals, hairs have evolved into sharp spines. The European hedgehog defends itself by rolling into a tight ball, while the much larger

Above: *Box-fish, or trunk-fish, are found in all the shallow seas of the tropics. These strange fish have double protection from predators. Their highly specialized scales form a hard shell-like covering over the head and body, and the fish also produces a poison.*

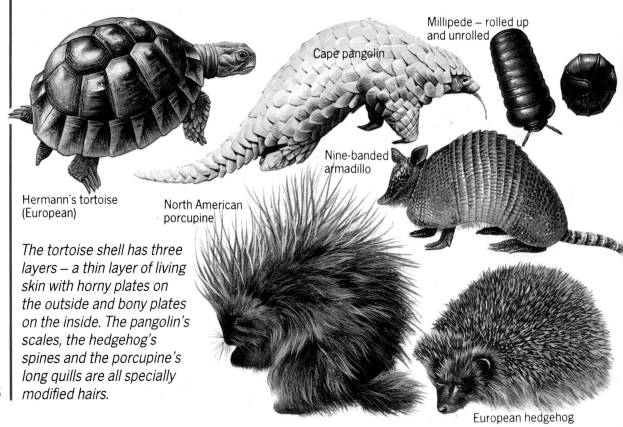

Millipede – rolled up and unrolled

Cape pangolin

Nine-banded armadillo

Hermann's tortoise (European)

North American porcupine

European hedgehog

The tortoise shell has three layers – a thin layer of living skin with horny plates on the outside and bony plates on the inside. The pangolin's scales, the hedgehog's spines and the porcupine's long quills are all specially modified hairs.

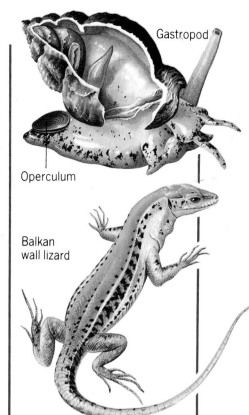

long-spined African porcupine has the alarming habit of rushing backwards straight at the face of its attacker. The spines of the much smaller tree-dwelling American porcupine are smaller, and hidden amongst its fur. But they contain a nasty surprise. The spines are very loosely attached, and an attacker is very likely to find itself with nothing but a mouthful of sharp spines when it tries to bite.

As a last resort, some animals are able to lose part of their body in an attack and still survive. Starfish, for example, can regrow an arm, while many lizards can cast off their tails in an attack and make their escape while the attacker's attention is on the twitching tail.

Nature's chemical warfare

One of the deadliest weapons in the animal world is poison – and it can be used just as well for defence as it can for attack. Many animals are protected by poisonous spines. They include bottom-dwelling fishes like stonefish and stargazers, burrowing worms like the green and red bristleworm, and countless 'hairy' caterpillars whose 'hairs' are really fine poison spines. Puffer fish and many beetles have poisonous chemicals in various parts of their bodies, while many other animals have poisons in their skin. These include the slimy-skinned soap-fishes, the famous arrow-poison frogs, and some of the gaudily-coloured sea slugs. Some sea slugs can even feed on sea anemones – and then build the anemone's poisonous sting cells into their own skin for their own protection!

Above: *The gastropod illustrated above can close its shell completely with a shelly plate called an operculum.*

The animal's body is lopsided and curiously twisted to fit inside the spiral shell.

Starfish and lizards are among the few animals that are able to regrow damaged parts of their bodies.

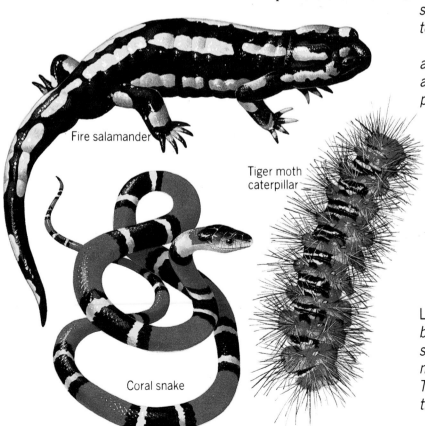

Left: *Brilliant colours may be attractive, but the ones shown here have a much more serious message. They are all warnings that their owners are poisonous.*

109

Colour, camouflage and trickery

Colours and shapes and patterns play a very important part in the battle for survival. They are used by hunters to improve their chances of success – and by the hunted in their constant struggle to avoid being caught.

The deadly game of hide and seek
The simplest way to conceal yourself in the forest, or in grassland or desert, is simply to match the colour of your surroundings, and many animals, especially the smaller ones, do just that. Many tropical tree snakes, frogs and lizards are bright green, shellfish are sandy coloured, grasshoppers are yellow or green, and wood-lice are the dull grey of wet earth and decaying leaves.

Patches or stripes of several different colours provide an even better disguise because the broken-up pattern of light and dark helps to hide the tell-tale outline of the animal's body, as well as helping it to merge into its background. The spotted coat of a baby deer is perfect **camouflage** against the bracken and leaves of a forest floor dappled with patches of sunlight shining through the trees overhead. In just the same way, patches and streaks of brown and black on a pale background make the eggs of plovers and terns and other shore birds almost impossible to see – even though they are laid right out in the open amongst the pebbles on a beach.

This kind of disguise also works for bigger animals. The most perfect camouflage of all is the striped coat of the tiger standing absolutely motionless in tall grass or the tangled undergrowth of a dry forest thicket.

Above: *The grasshopper's colour provides most of its protection, but its body shape, too, blends almost invisibly with the 'forest' of grass stems in which the insect lives.*

Below: *The black and orange stripes of the tiger's coat are perfect camouflage in the dry, golden colours of the undergrowth.*

The finest disguise of all is to combine colour and pattern and body shape so that the animal ceases to look like an animal at all. Stick insects and sea dragons, mantids and carpet sharks, all show this kind of camouflage in action. There is even an insect that is a perfect copy of a bird dropping!

Colours can also be used in self-defence – as a means of startling an attacker long enough for the victim to make a dash for safety. The dramatic eye-spots of the bush cricket (page 101) are just one example.

Nature's quick-change artists
For some animals, colour can be a bit of a problem. Butterflies, for example, need their bright colours in order to find each other during the brief mating period. But bright colours are also likely to make a resting butterfly an easy target for the first hungry bird that happens to come

Right: *Amongst animals, insects are the masters of disguise. They imitate every-* *thing from thorns to bird droppings to escape detection.*

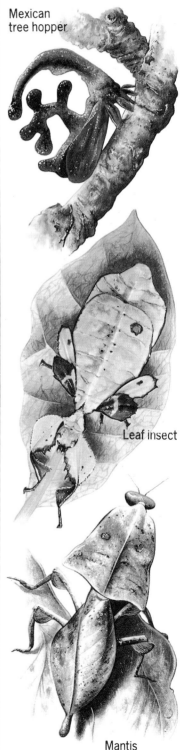

Left: *The stonefish is as dangerous as it is ugly. It lies motionless on the sea-bed, perfectly camouflaged, and its poisonous spines can inflict fatal injuries.*

Mexican tree hopper

Leaf insect

Mantis

along. Some common species such as the comma and the large tortoise-shell have solved this problem by having beautiful colours on their upper wing surfaces, clearly visible in flight, but drab 'dead leaf' colours on the under-sides which make them almost invisible the second they land and close their wings.

A few animals have even mastered the art of changing the colour of their skin in certain situations. Flat-fish such as sole and flounder can adjust their skin colour to match the sea-bed, although they can only do this slowly. Chameleons, too, can change colour to help them blend in with their surroundings. These changes are controlled by the brightness of the light, and by temperature, and by whether or not the animal is nervous or frightened.

Octopus, squid and cuttlefish have the most dramatic colour changes. They can do them very quickly, and also whenever they wish. Some changes are made to help disguise them when hunting, or when threatened by a predator, but some of the most spectacular colour changes are used in courtship displays. For example, to attract his mate, the male cuttle-fish ripples with waves of light and colour as colour cells in the skin are 'switched on and off' in quick succession.

Copy-cat trickery

The warning colours that are so common in poisonous animals also crop up again and again in an amazing variety of copy-cats and cheats who are not poisonous at all. This is especially common in insects, but obviously it cannot be

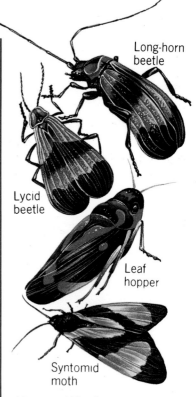

Above: *Which one is poisonous? That is the problem facing insect-eating birds in the forests of South America. In this group, the orange-banded lycid beetle is the dangerous one. The rest are edible 'mimics'. But how is the hunter to know?*

Above: *The comma butterfly is an attractive sight as the sun catches its upper wing colours in flight. But when the insect lands, its drab under-sides and ragged outline make it almost invisible.*

Above: *Like many lizards, the blue-tongued skink has bright contrasting colours on the tongue and inside the mouth, and these can be 'flashed' to distract an attacker long enough for the skink to escape.*

Above: *The skunk is quite harmless if left alone, but when threatened, it will defend itself by squirting a jet of foul-smelling liquid from glands beneath its tail. The trick usually drives off the attacker!*

deliberate copying as beetles, wasps and flies are not able to choose their own colours. It is something that has happened gradually as the various insect groups have evolved, and it works like this.

Insect-eating birds and other predators will normally attack any likely-looking insect they see. If the insect turns out to have sharp spines, or to squirt acid at its attacker, or to taste terrible, the bird will spit it out quickly. Now, if a large number of unpleasant-tasting insects also happen to have the same colouring – black and red, for example – the bird will gradually learn to associate those colours with a nasty experience and will leave black and red insects alone. The result is that most of the harmless black and red insects get left alone as well. These harmless copy-cats, or 'mimics' as they are called, are protected by the nasty reputation of their poisonous look-alikes.

Seasonal colour changes

As the days get shorter towards the end of summer, many animals of the temperate regions change from their light summer coats to thicker, warmer, winter fur or feathers. In the Arctic regions, some change the colour of their coats at the same time in order to conceal themselves in a landscape of snow and ice. Hunter and hunted alike shed the red and orange and brown tones of the summer and become almost completely white. The camouflage is perfect, but for the Arctic fox and the stoat (called ermine in winter) the silver-white fur has also made them a target for human hunters.

Below: Several northern forest animals such as bears and Arctic ground squirrels survive the winter by going into hibernation. The field vole (below), like shrews and lemmings, makes its winter burrow beneath the snow. Farther north the winter is so long and so cold that even this is not possible. The larger animals, such as caribou, elk and reindeer move south into the forests, always on the move in search of food. Others (bottom) remain active and continue the deadly game of hunter and hunted throughout the winter months.

Field vole

Arctic fox

Ptarmigan

Snowy owl

Arctic hare

The long-distance travellers

One of the first signs of spring in the temperate regions is the welcome return of the millions of birds that flew away at the end of the summer to spend the winter in some warmer part of the world. But birds are by no means the only travellers. In fact, most animals make regular journeys, called **migrations**, in search of food or to find the best place to have their young.

In the constantly warm, moist, tropical forests where food is plentiful all year round, very few animals need to migrate. But in the dry grasslands of Africa, huge herds of wildebeeste, zebra and gazelles are always moving across the plains, following the seasonal rains. Their young are born at the start of the main wet season, when food is in good supply, but right from the moment of birth they must keep up with the moving herd – or perish. At the other end of the world, caribou and reindeer spend the bitter Arctic winter in the forests of Canada and Asia, then migrate onto the open plains as the winter snows melt and the **tundra** is carpeted with mosses and lichens. Here their young are born, and by the end of the brief Arctic summer they too must be strong enough to follow the adults back to the safety of the forests.

For small insect-eaters and seed-eaters, food is scarce in the cold winter months so millions of them migrate from north Europe to the Mediterranean, or even as far as South Africa. The photograph above shows house martins gathering on telephone wires, preparing to leave.

A NATURAL TRAVELLER

Each year, in late April, the short-tailed shearwater leaves its nesting grounds in Tasmania and southeast Australia and heads out into the Pacific. For the next seven months it rides the great wind systems of that ocean, following the coast of Asia high into the Arctic regions, then swinging back south along the coasts of Canada and the USA before riding the trade winds back to its breeding grounds in the far south. It is a round trip of 32,000 kilometres – repeated year after year.

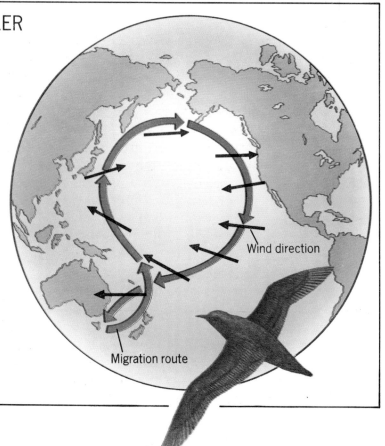

Wind direction

Migration route

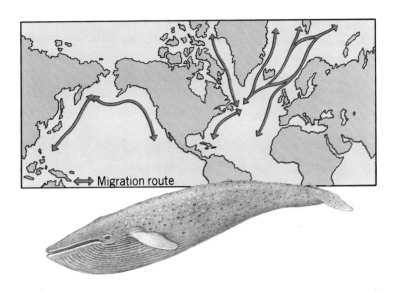

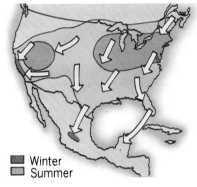

■ Winter
■ Summer

Above: *Each year, blue whales travel thousands of kilometres on their migrations. They feed in the rich Arctic waters in the summer, then travel to warmer waters for the winter, and to give birth to their young. Whales that summer in the North Pacific often travel as far as the Indian Ocean on their winter journeys.*

Above, photograph and small map: *The monarch butterfly of North America is the record-holder for insect migration. Butterflies that hatch in Canada in late summer fly up to 3000 kilometres to spend the winter in California, Texas or the mountains of Mexico.*

Birds are among the greatest travellers. Every year the Arctic tern covers a round trip of over 40,000 kilometres. The bird breeds in the Arctic but spends part of the year in the southern oceans fringing Antarctica. This remarkable traveller spends eight months of the year in non-stop flight, feeding as it goes by plunging down into the sea to catch its fish.

The oceans, too, have their share of record breakers. Many of the great whales spend a large part of the year feeding in the rich waters of the Arctic or Antarctic but travel thousands of kilometres to give birth to their young in the warmer waters of the tropics. The freshwater eels that live in the lakes and rivers of North America and Europe are all adults. They are born in the same small area of the western Atlantic, called the Sargasso Sea, and spend several years at sea before they make their way into the inland rivers. By contrast, salmon are spawned in upland rivers and do not make their way out to sea until they have grown to at least ten centimetres long. The fish then remain at sea for about four years before returning to the very same stream in which they were born.

Amongst the **reptiles** and **amphibians** only the marine turtles (page 76) and some sea snakes make long journeys, but many smaller members of the family make very short regular journeys in their breeding seasons. Adult toads will return every year to the same pond, making journeys of up to two kilometres, mainly at night and often over rough and difficult ground.

6. Our place in Nature

Animals and plants have been dying out quite naturally for millions of years. If this was not so, there would still be trilobites in the sea, tree-sized clubmosses covering parts of the land, and our modern birds would be sharing the skies with a variety of flying lizards. So, if becoming extinct is quite natural, why are scientists so concerned about 'endangered species' today?

The problem today is the way humans have completely taken over and dominated the natural world. A few animals will continue to die out naturally, but most of the animals and plants that are in danger today are threatened by us and not by natural events.

Some species are threatened by hunting. Crocodiles are hunted for their skins. Turtles are hunted for their meat. Whales are still hunted for their oil and meat. Some birds are hunted for their beautiful feathers while others are trapped and sold to collectors – so-called 'bird lovers' who will pay huge amounts of money for a single specimen of a very rare tropical forest parrot.

The biggest problem of all, however, is that many animals and plants are simply being pushed off the face of the Earth by people and their domestic animals. In 1970 there were less than four thousand million people on Earth. By the year 2000 there will be about six thousand million. They will all need food, and most will need wood to cook their food and build their houses. Already, some parts of the world have more people than the land can feed. Every year, enough tropical forest to cover the whole of England is cut down – most of it to make room for small farms to grow food for those people. The problem is that the soil beneath a tropical forest is not very fertile. It makes poor farmland. In a year or two the soil is exhausted, and most of it gets washed away in the rainy season.

Below: *The rosy periwinkle is a perfect example of the useful medicines that can be found in plants of the tropical forests.*

In this particular case, the plant was found to contain chemicals that helped in treating children with leukaemia.

The same kind of problems face the dry grassland areas of the world. Too many people and too many cattle and goats mean that all the grass is eaten, the scrub woodland is cut down for use as firewood, and in no time at all the grassland has turned into desert and people are starving. Even the high mountain regions cannot escape. In the Andes and Himalayas the hill forests are cut down for timber and firewood and the leafy hillside bushes are used to provide fodder for animals. But with the vegetation gone there is nothing to hold the thin soil in place. The first heavy rains wash it downhill into the valleys below. The rivers are blocked with silt, lowland areas are flooded, and even coastal fisheries can be ruined because of the mud carried into the sea. It is a perfect example of how everything in the natural world is linked. A tropical coral reef can be killed and a local fishing village lose its livelihood because of someone else's desperate need for firewood more than a thousand kilometres inland.

The reason why scientists and conservationists are so concerned today is that animals and plants are becoming extinct at a faster and faster rate. Take birds as an example. About 150 species have disappeared in the last 400 years, but at the present rate we could lose another 500 species by the year 2000. At present well over a thousand species are on the official 'Red List' of birds in

Above: *People must earn a living, so some forest trees must be cut for their timber. The danger comes when large areas are cleared of all their trees, because heavy rains soon wash away the fragile forest soil. Other threats to nature include dumping of chemicals in rivers and lakes* (above)*, and pollution of the air with dust and smoke.*

ENDANGERED SPECIES

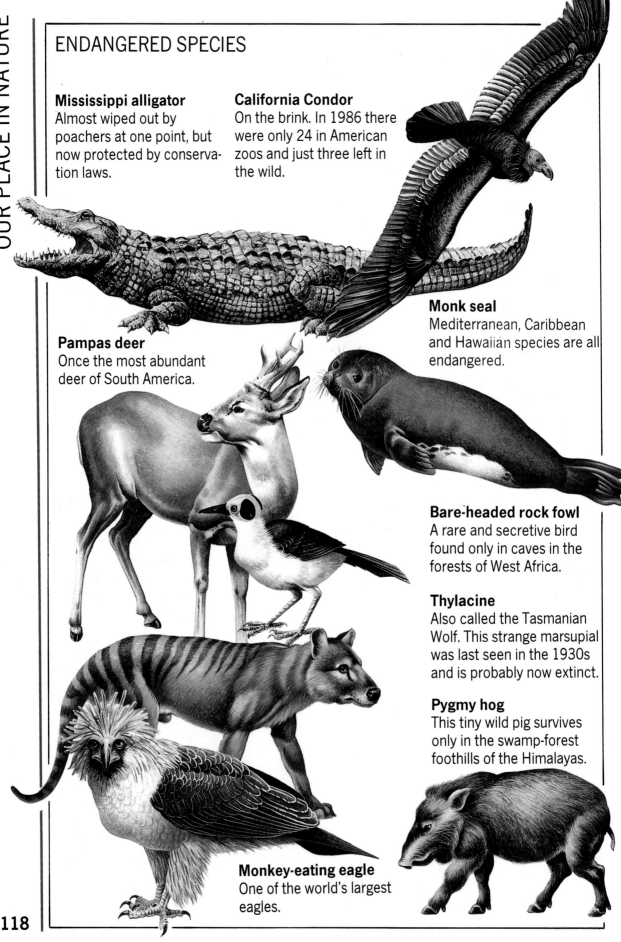

Mississippi alligator
Almost wiped out by poachers at one point, but now protected by conservation laws.

California Condor
On the brink. In 1986 there were only 24 in American zoos and just three left in the wild.

Monk seal
Mediterranean, Caribbean and Hawaiian species are all endangered.

Pampas deer
Once the most abundant deer of South America.

Bare-headed rock fowl
A rare and secretive bird found only in caves in the forests of West Africa.

Thylacine
Also called the Tasmanian Wolf. This strange marsupial was last seen in the 1930s and is probably now extinct.

Pygmy hog
This tiny wild pig survives only in the swamp-forest foothills of the Himalayas.

Monkey-eating eagle
One of the world's largest eagles.

danger. Because birds are relatively easy to study we have a lot of accurate information about them. Other animal groups have not been studied quite so well. Even so, biologists are now able to estimate that for every bird that is lost, the world also loses 80 or more insect species and between 30 and 40 plants. The tragedy of this is that so many of these plants could be important to our own future. We cannot breed new 'super crops' to feed the world if we destroy large numbers of plants before we have even studied them. But that is what is happening in the tropical forests. The great tropical rainforests also provide many of our most useful medicines, and they almost certainly hold many more life-saving drugs which we have not yet discovered.

The same thing is true of the oceans. They hold huge stocks of food, and many important minerals, including an amazing store of chemical substances that are not found on land. We probably know more about the far side of the Moon than we do about the chemistry of the deep oceans and the creatures that live there, yet we use them as a dumping ground for all kinds of waste. We spill oil into them. We allow industries to dump waste chemicals into them. But once in the sea these poisons spread right around the globe.

The future is in our hands

Conservation means much more than protecting rare animals. We saw earlier in this book that food chains and food webs, nutrient cycles and water cycles link all the world's plants and animals and habitats together. What happens in the future will affect us just as much as the rest of the animal world. The difference is that we are the only ones that can decide what happens. It is our world, and we are the ones who must look after it.

Above: *Conservation is for everyone. Here a group of conservation volunteers tackles the job of tidying a patch of scrub woodland to make a better habitat for wild plants and animals.*

Below: *The peace and stillness of a quiet evening at Minsmere in Great Britain – one of the main bird reserves owned and run by the Royal Society for the Protection of Birds.*

Glossary

Words in SMALL CAPITALS have their own separate glossary entry.

Abdomen In most animals this is the lower part of the body. It contains the stomach and intestines. In insects it is the last of the three body sections.

Adaptation The slow process of change that adjusts an animal to fit into a particular set of living conditions.

Amphibian An animal that lives part of its life in water and part on land. The amphibians are part-way between the REPTILES and the fishes.

Axolotl

Bacterium (plural bacteria) A microscopic single-celled plant. Most are harmless, but some cause diseases. Bacteria play an important part in breaking down dead plant and animal remains.

Blubber The thick layer of fat under the skin of a whale or seal.

Bulb The thick, round base of the stem of some plants such as lilies and onions. The bulb sends down roots and sends up shoots to produce a new plant.

Camouflage Disguise, produced by colour or pattern or shape, which makes an animal hard to see.

Canopy The main leafy layer in a forest. In the canopy, branches of neighbouring trees overlap, forming an almost continuous 'roof' high above the ground.

Carrion Dead flesh. The remains of an animal that has died.

Cartilage the tough, elastic gristle in animal bodies. A layer of cartilage makes joints work smoothly. In sharks, the SKELETON is made entirely of this material, and not of bone.

Cell The smallest living unit. Animals and plants are built of cells. Some may have just one. Others, such as humans, are made of many. A human adult has about 60 million million cells.

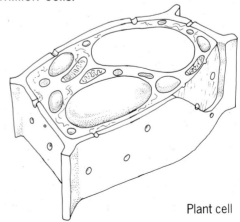

Plant cell

Chlorophyll The green chemical that gives plants their colour. It enables a plant cell to capture the energy in the Sun's rays and turn it into food.

Chloroplast The tiny packages inside a plant cell that contain the CHLOROPHYLL.

Clutch The set of eggs laid by a bird.

Cold-blooded The term used to describe an animal that cannot automatically keep its body at operating temperature by burning fuel (sugar) stored in the body. A cold-blooded animal remains at about the same temperature as its surroundings.

Colony A large number of animals living together. Ants, rabbits, seals and gulls all live in colonies.

Conifer Any kind of tree that has cones.

Corm A thickened underground stem, very like a bulb except that it is solid, not made of layers. Common example is crocus.

Courtship The behaviour that leads up to two animals pairing off and MATING.

Deciduous A tree that sheds all or most of its leaves at roughly the same time every year. It is the opposite of evergreen.

Dicotyledon A plant that starts off with two tiny leaves when it first sprouts from the SEED.

Display Any kind of animal behaviour that has a particular meaning. Courtship display is used to attract a mate; threat display to frighten off an enemy, and so on.

Ecosphere The region around the Sun where it is neither too hot, nor too cold, for life to exist.

Evolution The changes that take place in animals and plants, very slowly, bit by bit, over millions of years.

Food chain The natural links between animals and what they eat. A simple example is cat-bird-spider-fly – each one eats the next one down the chain.

Fossil The remains of an animal or plant, or its imprint, left in the rocks of the earth's surface. The best fossils are found in limestone and mudstone.

Fossil of ginkgo leaf

Fruit The fleshy part of a plant, which forms a container for the SEEDS.

Fungus A large family of 'plants' that includes mushrooms, toadstools, moulds, and the plate-like crusts that grow on woodland trees. They are not true plants as they contain no CHLOROPHYLL.

Gill The breathing organ of an animal that lives in water. It takes oxygen from the water just as an animal's lung takes oxygen from the air.

Habitat The natural living place of an animal or plant. Examples are ponds, woodland, grassland, desert.

Hibernate To spend the winter in a kind of deep sleep. The animal slows down its heartbeat and other body systems and lives off stored body fat until the spring.

Host An animal or plant that is used by another animal or plant as a source of food. The PARASITE lives on, or in some cases inside, the host.

Instinct A built-in ability to do certain things without having to learn them or be shown. Baby turtles instinctively head for the sea as soon as they hatch out.

Intelligence Quickness of mind, or ability to think and work things out.

Invertebrate An animal that does not have a backbone.

Larva The grub of an insect. The insect is a larva from the moment it hatches from the egg until the time it turns into a pupa. (The

121

final stage is when the adult insect emerges from the pupa.)

Mammal An animal that gives birth to live young and feeds the baby on milk produced in the mother's body.

Marsupial A group of primitive mammals whose babies are born at a very early stage but then finish off their development in a pouch on the mother's abdomen.

Mating season The time of year when male and female animals pair off, or gather in groups, in order to breed.

Metamorphosis The word means 'change of shape' and it describes the changes in an insect's life from egg to LARVA to pupa and finally to adult. At each change, the insect grows a totally new kind of body.

Migrate Make a regular journey to a particular place in order to breed and raise young, or in some cases to search out better food supplies.

Molecule The smallest particle of a substance that can exist on its own. For example, a molecule of water is made of one atom of oxygen joined to two atoms of hydrogen.

Monocotyledon A plant that starts off with just one tiny leaf when it first sprouts from the SEED.

Natural selection A natural process in which the animals best equipped for a particular set of living conditions will be the most successful breeders. Their good features are therefore passed on to the new generation.

Nectar A sugary solution produced by certain parts of some flowers. It is the main food for many kinds of insects.

Nocturnal Active at night.

Nucleus The central part of an animal or plant cell which acts as a command centre and controls all the chemical processes the cell carries out.

Ovary The tough case in the middle of a flower that contains and protects the eggs (OVULES). It is the ovary that usually swells

and forms the FRUIT of the plant when it has been fertilized.

Ovule The egg CELL of a plant. When it has been fertilized it becomes a SEED.

Parasite A plant or animal that depends completely on another plant or animal in order to stay alive.

Photosynthesis The word means 'building with light'. It is the chemical process that takes place in green leaves. Water and carbon dioxide from the air are used to make sugars that are the main plant food. The process uses energy from the Sun.

Different pollen shapes

Pollen The male CELLS of a plant. When pollen is carried by the wind or by an insect to another plant, that plant may be fertilized. Then it can produce SEEDS that will grow into new plants.

Primate The very advanced group of MAMMALS that is our own immediate family. The group includes apes, monkeys, humans, lemurs and tarsiers.

Protozoan A member of the simplest of all animal groups – the primitive single-celled animals.

Chimpanzee

Reproduction The process of making new members of the same animal or plant SPECIES. Some species reproduce asexually, just by growing an additional replica of the parent, or by splitting into two identical copies. Others reproduce sexually, that is by joining together an egg from a female parent and SPERM from the male parent.

Reptile A group of cold-blooded animals that lay eggs on land. A few give birth to live young.

Rhizome A stem that grows along just under the surface of the ground. It can produce buds which can then sprout up through the ground and form new plants.

Rodent An animal of the mouse-squirrel-beaver-porcupine family. All rodents have big, chisel-like front teeth which they use for gnawing tough plant food.

Roost The place where bats or birds go to sleep. The word is also a verb – most birds roost in trees or on town buildings.

Ruminant An animal like a cow, goat or sheep that has a four-chambered stomach which enables it to process tough plant food. Ruminants feed, then later they cough up the food and chew it a second time. It is called chewing the cud.

Runner A stem that grows along on top of the ground and puts down roots every so often. A common example is the strawberry plant.

Saliva The juice that is produced by glands in the mouth. It helps to soften food and make it slide down easily, but it also contains important chemicals that start the process of digesting the food.

Seed A small capsule containing a baby plant and a small store of food to give it a start in life.

Skeleton The framework of bone or CARTIL-AGE that supports the body of a bird, MAMMAL, fish, AMPHIBIAN or REPTILE. Crabs, insects and some other animals wear their skeletons *outside* – in the form of a shell or horny outer layer.

Species A group of animals of the same kind, which can breed and produce more of their own kind. A robin, for example, is one species of bird, while a blackbird is a different species.

Sperm The male sex CELLS, which combine with the female egg cell to fertilize it and so enable it to grow into a new plant or animal.

Spore The reproductive CELL of certain plants. Fungi, for example, reproduce by producing spores which drift on the wind and grow wherever they land.

Territory A patch of ground that an animal (usually but not always the male) takes over and claims as his own.

Thorax The middle section of an insect's body, between the head and the ABDOMEN. The abdomen carries three pairs of legs and two pairs of wings.

Insect

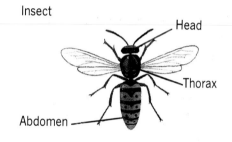

Head

Thorax

Abdomen

Tuber The swollen end of an underground stem, which can sprout to produce new plants. The most common example is the potato plant.

Tundra The region between the cold northern forests and the polar desert of bare rock, ice and snow. It is a region of thin soil which is always frozen, apart from the surface layer, which melts in summer so that a carpet of grass and lichen can grow.

Vertebrate An animal with a backbone.

Warm-blooded An animal that can maintain its body at full operating temperature by burning fuel (food) to create chemical energy. Warm-blooded animals can keep themselves warm in cold weather (within certain limits) and cool in hot weather.

Index

Page numbers in *italics*
refer to pictures

125

Acknowledgements

Page **4** B. Davidson/Survival Anglia; **6** M. Fogden/Bruce Coleman; **7** Swift Picture Library; **12** Imitor; **18** S. Dalton/NPHA; **20** Natonal Trust; **23** J & D. Bartlett/Bruce Coleman; **25** Swift Picture Library; **27** ZEFA; **29** S. Dalton/NHPA; **33** Swift Picture Library; **34** (left) L. Campbell/NHPA, (right) E. Murtomäki/NHPA; **35** A.I. Bernard/NHPA; **37** J. Shaw/NHPA; **42** Swift Picture Library; **45** ZEFA; **46** L. Campbell/NHPA; **49** Oxford Scientific Films Stills; **53** A. Bannister/NHPA; **57** Swift Picture Library; **58** A. Bannister/NHPA; **59** J. Shaw/NHPA; **61** (top) A. Bannister/NHPA, (bottom) ZEFA; **62** NHPA; **65** Swift Picture Library; **71** Carl Roessler/Planet Earth Pictures; **73** Oxford Scientific Stills; **77** ZEFA; **78** Dr F. Koster/Survival Anglia; **80** Imitor; **82** NHPA; **83** Swift Picture Library; **84** S.J. Krasemann/NHPA; **85** L.H. Newman/NHPA; **86** G. Ziesler/Bruce Coleman; **90** N. Myers/Bruce Coleman; **92** ZEFA; **94** I. Polunin/NHPA; **96** J & D Bartlett/Survival Anglia; **98** B. Davidson/Survival Anglia; **100** Bruce Coleman; **102** C. Hughes/Bruce Coleman; **110** G. Ziesler/Bruce Coleman; **111** ARDEA; **114** B. Hawkes/NHPA; **115** ARDEA; **116** ARDEA; **117** (top) L.C. Marigo/Bruce Coleman, (middle right) J. Foott/Survival Anglia; **119** (top and bottom) Swift Picture Library.